822·33

New Casebooks

MACBETH

New Casebooks

PUBLISHED
Hamlet
Middlemarch
Tristram Shandy
Macbeth

FORTHCOMING
Emma
Sense and Sensibility and *Pride and Prejudice*
Jane Eyre
Wuthering Heights
Villette
Great Expectations
Tess of the D'Urbervilles
Jude The Obscure
To the Lighthouse and *Mrs Dalloway*
Sons and Lovers
Ulysses
Waiting for Godot and *Endgame*
Chaucer
Metaphysical Poetry
Wordsworth
Blake
Shakespeare's History Plays
King Lear
Antony and Cleopatra

New Casebooks

MACBETH

WILLIAM SHAKESPEARE

EDITED BY ALAN SINFIELD

MACMILLAN

First published 1992 by
MACMILLAN EDUCATION LTD
Houndmills, Basingstoke, Hampshire RG21 2XS
and London
Companies and representatives
throughout the world

ISBN 0–333–54442–0 hardcover
ISBN 0–333–54443–9 paperback

A catalogue record for this book is available
from the British Library.

Printed in Hong Kong

Contents

Acknowledgements   vii

General Editors' Preface   ix

Introduction: ALAN SINFIELD   1

 1. *Macbeth* and Masculine Values   14
    MARILYN FRENCH

 2. *Macbeth* and Witchcraft   25
    PETER STALLYBRASS

 3. The Character of Lady Macbeth   39
    SIGMUND FREUD

 4. 'The witches are the heroines of the piece . . .'   46
    TERRY EAGLETON

 5. 'Born of woman': Fantasies of Maternal Power in *Macbeth*   53
    JANET ADELMAN

 6. Imperfect Speakers: the Tale Thickens   69
    MALCOLM EVANS

 7. Subjectivity and the Soliloquy   79
    CATHERINE BELSEY

 8. Speculations: *Macbeth* and Source   92
    JONATHAN GOLDBERG

 9. Lying like Truth: Riddle, Representation, and Treason in
    Renaissance England   108
    STEVEN MULLANEY

10. *Macbeth*: History, Ideology and Intellectuals   121
    ALAN SINFIELD

11. Tragedy and Literature   136
    JONATHAN DOLLIMORE

12. Radical Potential: *Macbeth* on Film   151
    GRAHAM HOLDERNESS

Further Reading   161

Notes on Contributors   166

Index   169

Acknowledgements

The editor and publishers wish to thank the following for permission to use copyright material:

Janet Adelman, extracts from 'Born of Woman: fantasies of maternal power in *Macbeth*' in *Cannibals, Witches and Divorce: Estranging the Rennaissance*, ed. Marjorie Garber (1987), by permission of Johns Hopkins University Press;

Catherine Belsey, extracts from *The Subject of Tragedy*, Methuen & Co (1985), by permission of Routledge;

Jonathan Dollimore, extracts from *Radical Tragedy* (1984), by permission of Harvester-Wheatsheaf and University of Chicago Press;

Malcolm Evans, extract from *Signifying Nothing*, 2nd edn (1989), by permission of Harvester-Wheatsheaf and University of Georgia Press, copyright © 1986 by Malcolm Evans;

Terry Eagleton, extract from *William Shakespeare* (1986), by permission of Basil Blackwell Ltd;

Marilyn French, extract from *Shakespeare's Division of Experience* (1982), by permission of Jonathan Cape Ltd and Charlotte Sheedy, Literary Agency, Inc. on behalf of the author;

Sigmund Freud, extract from 'Some Character-Types Met within Psychoanalytical Work' in *The Standard Edition of the Complete Psychological Works*, vol. 14, ed. James Strachey, Hogarth Press and the Institute of Psycho-Analysis (1957), by permission of Random Century Group and Basic Books Inc.;

Jonathan Goldberg, extracts from 'Speculations: *Macbeth* and

Source' in *Shakespeare Reproduced*, eds J. E. Howard and M. F. O'Connor, Methuen & Co. (1987), by permission of Routledge;

Graham Holderness, 'Radical Potentiality and Institutional Closure' in *Political Shakespeare*, eds Jonathan Dollimore and Alan Sinfield (1985), by permission of Manchester University Press;

Steven Mullaney, extracts from 'The Place of the Stage', *English Literary History*, 47 (1980), by permission of Johns Hopkins University Press;

Alan Sinfield, extracts from '*Macbeth*: history, ideology and intellectuals', *Critical Quarterly*, 28, Nos. 1, 2 (1986), by permission of the author;

Peter Stallybrass, extracts from '*Macbeth* and Witchcraft' in *Focus on Macbeth*, ed. John Russell Brown (1982), by permission of Routledge.

Every effort has been made to trace all the copyright holders but if any have been inadvertently overlooked the publishers will be pleased to make the necessary arrangement at the first opportunity.

General Editors' Preface

The purpose of this new series of Casebooks is to reveal some of the ways in which contemporary criticism has changed our understanding of commonly studied texts and writers and, indeed, of the nature of criticism itself. Central to the series is a concern with modern critical theory and its effect on current approaches to the study of literature. Each New Casebook editor has been asked to select a sequence of essays which will introduce the reader to the new critical approaches to the text or texts being discussed in the volume and also illuminate the rich interchange between critical theory and critical practice that characterises so much current writing about literature.

The series itself, of course, grows out of the original Casebook series edited by A. E. Dyson. The original volumes provide readers with a range of critical opinions extending from the first reception of a work through to the criticism of the twentieth century. By contrast, the focus of the New Casebooks is on modern critical thinking and practice, with the volumes seeking to reflect both the controversy and the excitement of current criticism. Because much of this criticism is difficult and often employs an unfamiliar critical language, editors have been asked to give the reader as much help as they feel is appropriate, but without simplifying the essays or the issues they raise.

The project of the New Casebooks, then, is to bring together in an illuminating way those critics who best illustrate the ways in which contemporary criticism has established new methods of analysing texts and who have reinvigorated the important debate about how we 'read' literature. The hope is, of course, that New Casebooks will not only open up this debate to a wider audience, but will also encourage students to extend their own ideas, and think afresh about their responses to the texts they are studying.

John Peck and Martin Coyle
University of Wales, Cardiff

Introduction

ALAN SINFIELD

Willy Russell's play *Educating Rita* has two characters: Frank, a university teacher, and Rita who comes to study with him for an Open University examination. She is lively and straightforward, but has no background in English Literature (for her 'Yeats' is not a poet but a local wine bar); it looks as if she will not get on too well. A turning point is when she goes to see *Macbeth* and rushes to tell Frank about it (read her with a Liverpudlian accent):

> It was Shakespeare, I thought it was gonna be dead borin'. . . . But listen, it wasn't borin', it was bleedin' great, honest, ogh, it done me in, it was fantastic. I'm gonna do an essay on it. . . . Wasn't his wife a cow, eh? An' that fantastic bit where he meets Macduff an' he thinks he's all invincible. I was on the edge of me seat at that bit. I wanted to shout out an' tell Macbeth, warn him. . . . It was like a thriller.[1]

Frank explains the traditional literary-critical approach to *Macbeth* and tragedy, and from this point Rita hardly looks back.

In the film made in 1983 (with Michael Caine and Julie Walters) the *Macbeth* incident is carefully set up: Rita appears running through the streets to urgent music, while Frank is talking to his class of regular students about the tragic hero. Rita searches for him in his study, runs down to the lecture room, looks in through the window: she is plainly the outsider. She tells Frank of her excitement at the play, and he takes her into the lecture room; the students all look round. He continues with his lecture, saying how the academic idea of tragedy differs from the popular: 'Man Killed By Falling Tree', in a newspaper headline, is not properly about tragedy. 'It is for the poor sod under the tree', Rita chips in, and the students laugh.[2] Frank's main difficulty has been explaining to Rita that literature differs from other books (she thinks 'they were all good in their own

1

way').[3] The defining of tragedy as a special experience is central to the defining of literature as a special experience. The exchange marks the boundary between popular and academic ideas; it is the point at which one might want a New Casebook on *Macbeth*.

TRAGEDY

Frank says he is an appalling teacher, and eventually he is asked to leave his job after lecturing while drunk. But it turns out that he has been good for Rita because he has taken an interest in her for herself and allowed her space in which to develop her own thoughts. However, on tragedy and *Macbeth* Frank has not taken account of recent ideas – his approach belongs to the start rather than the close of the twentieth century, deriving from A. C. Bradley's *Shakespearean Tragedy*, first published in 1904. Frank is close to Bradley when he says:

> Macbeth is flawed by his ambition – yes? . . . it's that flaw which forces him to take the inevitable steps towards his own doom. You see? . . . the sort of thing you read in the paper as being tragic, 'Man Killed By Falling Tree', is not a tragedy. . . . Tragedy in dramatic terms is inevitable, pre-ordained. . . . You see [Macbeth] goes blindly on and on and with every step he's spinning one more piece of thread which will eventually make up the network of his own tragedy.[4]

Behind this is the idea of 'tragedy' as a universal form, embodying the specially noble experience of elite individuals who create their own doom within an overarching framework of mysterious inevitability. This kind of approach was challenged by Raymond Williams in his book *Modern Tragedy* (1966). Williams reviews the diverse kinds of tragedy that have been written and written about and shows how they derive from quite different cultures. The literary-critical idea of tragedy depends upon 'the assumption of a permanent, universal and essentially unchanging human nature' which all tragedies, from the Greeks to Ibsen, have intuited. If we do not hold that assumption, and Williams does not, then tragedy becomes

> not a single and permanent kind of fact, but a series of experiences and conventions and institutions. It is not a case of interpreting this series by reference to a permanent and unchanging human nature. Rather, the varieties of tragic experience are to be interpreted by reference to the changing conventions and institutions.[5]

In the light of this argument, Frank's Bradleyan approach manifests not a profound truth, but a conservative attempt to hold the concept of tragedy to a traditional, literary-critical interpretation.

The issue is not who is right, but who is claiming authority over concepts and which interests are being served. Williams believes that withholding tragedy from ordinary people is a way of disqualifying their experience and feeding an elitism which is ultimately social, economic and political. He says: 'in the case of ordinary death and suffering, when we see mourning and lament, when we see men and women breaking under their actual loss, it is at least not self-evident to say that we are not in the presence of tragedy.'[6] It is often said that there are no modern tragedies; the reason is that 'tragedy' has been defined in a way which rules out the overwhelming proportion of potential modern instances. Of course, there is a basic contradiction here, for tragedy is offered as both a universal experience of 'man' and as absent from our societies. What is really being said, I think, is that the modern world is an undignified place, lacking the highest kind of humanity, because all these ordinary people don't sufficiently defer to the ruling elite but instead expect their needs to be taken seriously.

The counter-argument used to be that the deaths of political leaders matter more than those of other people. Hence in part the notion that tragedy is 'inevitable, pre-ordained': this derives from societies which believed in a god or gods and that he or they took special interest in the 'fate' of the ruling elite (whereas the man under the tree merely suffers an accident). Interestingly, Frank does not say that – neither he nor Willy Russell, I think, expects most of us today to accept that top people as such have nobler kinds of experiences. Indeed, Frank is hardly able to answer Rita's rejection of the novel *Howards End* on the ground that E. M. Forster says there: 'We are not concerned with the poor'.[7] Instead Frank, like A. C. Bradley, derives tragic nobility and inevitability from the hero's qualities: he has a 'particular flaw in his character that has dictated his end', whereas if the man killed by a falling tree had 'been warned of the consequences of standing beneath that particular tree he wouldn't have done it, would he?'[8] It is not hard to answer Frank's point. For instance, every year hundreds of people are killed driving vehicles when they have drunk too much alcohol, despite being warned. We could say that all these drivers had flaws in their characters and therefore are tragic, but most traditional theorists would not want to do that. They would probably insist that Macbeth still displays a distinctive spiritual nobility which puts him above ordinary people.[9]

The fundamental trouble with the specialised notion of tragedy, Williams observes, is that it makes suffering seem to belong to 'man' rather than to society. We have plenty of suffering today – 'war, revolution, poverty, hunger; men reduced to objects and killed from lists; persecution and torture' – but in the Bradleyan idea of tragedy all these seem insignificant beside 'the fault in the soul'.[10] Actually, a good deal of suffering is produced through the human societies which we have organised through our human histories, and it is in these societies that suffering may be addressed – where the world may be changed. The Bradleyan idea of tragedy acts to inhibit us from seeing this: the flaw is in 'man' and changing the world would not help. In Brecht's *The Good Person of Szechwan*, a purposefully non-tragic play, Wang suggests to the gods that annual floods in the province may have occurred because the people are not god-fearing. The Second God replies: 'Rubbish. Because they didn't look after the dam properly'.[11]

Williams's account of the metaphysics of tragedy is taken further by Jonathan Dollimore in the eleventh piece in this collection (*Macbeth* is not discussed specifically by Dollimore here, but the argument is very relevant to the play). Dollimore locates the traditional conception of tragedy in 'essentialist humanism', elaborates the pattern of ideas and values which has made it so powerful in parts of modern culture, and then expounds an anti-humanist or cultural-materialist theory of subjectivity. The displacement of 'man' from the centre of the universe is traced from Copernicus through Darwin, Marx and Freud: the human subject is to be understood not as an autonomous, self-determining centre of consciousness, but as informed by social and ideological processes.

GENDER

Gender and sexual politics probably have a more immediate appeal, which is why they come first in the present collection of essays. Here too, social and political questions are often to the fore in recent criticism. Lady Macbeth has often been regarded as not merely murderous, like her husband, but distinctively demonic. Macbeth, Marilyn French remarks (essay 1 below), is presented as violating moral law, but Lady Macbeth seems to violate natural law: she is unfeminine. Rita's comment, 'Wasn't his wife a cow, eh?' is amusing because it undercuts the mystique of 'evil' which has enveloped Lady Macbeth, but at the expense of retaining a traditional image of the woman who speaks out of place. Frank says nothing of 'evil': his approach is humanistic, and for him demonic possession would be a rather embarrassing feature of the play. However, he does not remark on the sexism in Rita's 'cow' comment: in this, again, he is a conservative critic. For Marilyn French, Rita's way of thinking about a purposeful woman is recognisable enough, but not inevitable. It is one facet of an oppressive pattern of gender relations in *Macbeth* and in much of modern society. Peter Stallybrass (essay 2) takes this further, arguing that the witches in the play are not a *reflection* of the way the world is, but a key factor in a particular conceptualisation of social and political order. Witchcraft, Stallybrass shows, drawing upon anthropological modes of interpretation, was associated in Shakespeare's time with 'unnatural' female dominance and the overthrow of patriarchal authority. The witches and Lady Macbeth together form a pattern of perverted femininity which is in conflict with, yet required for, the legitimation of the ruling elite.

Freud's thoughts on Lady Macbeth (essay 3) are significant, in my view, not because they are especially psychoanalytic, but because that astute observer finds the character of Lady Macbeth unconvincing. Why, Freud asks, does she start off so remorseless and end up borne down by remorse? The usual explanation is that Lady Macbeth has an originally, naturally, gentle and womanly nature, and therefore collapses from the strain of violating that nature. But Freud explicitly dismisses this idea (and is driven to suggest that Lady Macbeth and Macbeth may be two parts of a single split personality; I do not think this latter idea is very useful). What Freud helps us to see is that critics have made Lady Macbeth plausible by fitting her into a sexist scenario which says that strength and determination in women are unnatural and can be developed only at a cost, such that their eventual failure is at once inevitable, natural, a punishment and a warning.

Terry Eagleton (in essay 4) suggests, provocatively, that the play, without knowing it, is on the side of the witches. Drawing implicitly upon Mikhail Bakhtin's idea of carnival as (among other things) the riot of unsocialised language,[12] Eagleton declares that the witches constitute an alternative sisterhood hovering at the margins of the Scottish polity, undermining its ethos of routine oppression and continuous warfare with their fertile, riddling speech. Lady Macbeth,

Eagleton adds, is different from the witches: she too scorns the male
ethos, but where they undermine it she, a prototype of the modern
bourgeois individualist, tries to seize it for herself. For all these
writers on gender, the corollary of Lady Macbeth's special kind of
femininity is an anxiety in the play about Macbeth's 'manliness'.
Janet Adelman's essay (number 5 below) centres around a perception
of male vulnerability in respect of the mothering power of women.
From an explicitly psychoanalytical perspective, Adelman teases out
the intricate shape of a defensive male fantasy which the play both
repudiates and enacts. Like many recent critics, Adelman finds that
Macbeth brings gender roles and boundaries into question.

STRUCTURALISM AND POSTSTRUCTURALISM

Frank speaks of Macbeth as if he were an actual person – as Bradley
tended to do. In Adelman's analysis, characters, incidents and images
may exchange gender, combine, metamorphose into, substitute for,
reconstitute and double each other. These are the analytic modes of
structuralism and poststructuralism. Like the other commentators
here, Adelman does not assume that the characters are actual people;
rather, they are textual arrangements which involve ideas about
people. They do not represent a centred, settled human reality, but a
strategic organisation tending to construct a particular interpretation
of the world. Structuralism, in brief, is concerned to locate such
organising patterns. It holds that identity and meaning are relational:
they depend not on the intrinsic identities of things as such, but on
the connections and disjunctions between them; we construct our
world through language systems which set concepts in a pattern of
mutually defining relations. Poststructuralism, equally briefly, starts
from the same point but does not expect the patterns to be stable;
on the contrary, it expects them always to be sliding away, even
as they are apprehended; no textual project can contain all the
meaning that it produces. The critics discussed so far draw upon
a range of recent intellectual work – philosophical materialism,
anthropology, psychoanalysis – but they are all structuralists or
poststructuralists.

This is the key difference between the essays collected here and
traditional criticism: the latter tries characteristically to discover
coherence – that the text constitutes an organic whole, is formally
complete, makes sense, works, gels, has a beginning, middle and end.

In the traditional speculation about character motivation, image patterns, thematic integration, structure, the task always was to fill in the gaps, to explain away the awkward points, resolve the cruces; to retell the story so that it makes more cogent or more acceptable sense – in short, to help the text into coherence. And the discovery of coherence was taken as the demonstration of quality. For poststructuralism, the better move is to dwell upon the awkward, unresolved points in the text, using them to open up its narrative strategies to critical questioning.[13]

The passage by Malcolm Evans printed here (essay 6) is virtually an illustration of a poststructuralist awareness of language and culture. Evans hears two linguistic modes in *Macbeth*: an unequivocal idiom of linguistic fullness and competence in which the divine legitimation of Duncan is announced, and a negating undertow in which the inescapable intractability of language intimates a more deeply rooted disorder. In Eagleton's account this latter is the language especially of the witches; for Evans, it infects all the dialogue.

The radical instability of language and identity is the theme also of Catherine Belsey (essay 7). Frank in *Educating Rita*, like Bradley and many traditional critics, assumes that in some sense Macbeth determines his own fate. For them, ambition is a facet of Macbeth's character; he possesses a coherent, individual subjectivity which makes him the kind of person he is; and this is the source of meaning and truth in the play. But how coherent is the subjectivity of any person? – this is the question that recent criticism pursues. Belsey argues that 'man' and 'the individual' are concepts created in history; we imagine ourselves to be free-standing individuals, and this suits the dominant ideology of Western liberal democracy (compare Dollimore's account of essentialist humanism). Belsey shows how drama during Shakespeare's lifetime, particularly in the development of the soliloquy, discarded allegory and morality personifications and found ways to suggest that the important conflicts occur within the mind of the protagonist. However, the subjectivities presented by Dr Faustus, Lady Macbeth and Macbeth retain signs of fragmentation and discontinuity.

Jonathan Goldberg finds a comparable instability in the text itself (essay 8). Until recently, the goal of most textual scholarship was to establish the proper words of Shakespearean plays; now it is often said that this is a chimera, and that the playtexts are ineradicably unstable. *King Lear*, for instance, has been found to exist in two distinct versions, each of a certain provenance.[14] Goldberg shows that the words spoken by Duncan and Macbeth come from diverse parts of Holinshed's *Chronicles*, bearing with them disturbing traces of their origins; so the text is unstable in relation to its source. Also, it is in uncertain relation with its occasion, in that King James seems neither quite outside nor quite inside the text. Like Eagleton, Goldberg believes that the witches embody this kind of indeterminacy, figuring an alternative to assertive masculine power.

POLITICS

Frank, in *Educating Rita*, fails to counter Rita's belief that if literature ignores the poor, the powerless, then so much the worse for literature.[15] It has frequently been acknowledged that *Macbeth* refers, indeed defers, to the contemporary political situation, with James VI of Scotland becoming James I of England. And until recently a hierarchical 'order' of the state, nature and divinity, to which the play alludes, was most often admired as a wise vision of how 'man' should live in the world. For the critics discussed so far, the political implications are quite different. Stallybrass, Eagleton, Evans and Goldberg delight in observing that this official ideology cannot secure itself against subversion; Dollimore and Belsey critique its metaphysical basis; and for Marilyn French, Macbeth is as much a butcher at the start as at the end because he is acting within the demands of a masculine culture.

Critics who take the traditional view – admiring the 'order' implied in *Macbeth* – tend to suggest that the play and the 'order' are timeless, whereas those who aspire to critique such a politics are likely to set both play and 'order' in a historical context. In North America especially, those doing the latter are often located within a critical framework known as 'new historicism'. This historicism is 'new' in that it draws upon the range of theoretical innovations I have been describing; it neither seeks nor admires the formal completeness which traditionally was discovered in art, tragedy and Jacobean monarchical ideology. Deconstruction of metaphysics converges upon critique of the pretensions of ruling elites and the state. New historicism focuses upon the production of ideology through representation; often it remarks the theatricality through which the state manifests its power, and sets it alongside the power which passes through the theatre. As Stephen Mullaney observes (essay 9), the actors' stage is like those upon which monarchs paraded in triumph and criminals were exhibited for torture and death. In Mullaney's argument the linguistic instability which undermined univocal monarchical power – and specially riddles, equivocations and prophecies like those of the witches – is found to have been associated in Shakespeare's time with treasonous thought and behaviour.

New historists are very often concerned, as Don Wayne suggests, with

> how different kinds of discourse intersect, contradict, destabilise, cancel, or modify each other ... seek[ing] to demonstrate how a dominant ideology will give a certain rein to alternative discourses, ultimately appropriating their vitality and containing their oppositional force.[16]

Of course, not all work generally dubbed 'new historicist' takes this line, but it is often argued that dissidence is always contained, in the very processes of language and power that give it voice. Cultural materialism, which has developed mainly in Britain and owes more to Raymond Williams and a European Marxist and socialist tradition, aspires to theorise more scope for dissidence. My own essay here (number 10; see also Dollimore's, number 11) argues that a split between legitimacy and actual power was likely in the Jacobean state; that the distinction between the lawful, good king (such as Duncan appears to be) and the usurping tyrant (such as Macbeth appears to be) was always uneasy; that other theories of the state were current; and that these other theories may help to provoke alternative, dissident interpretive possibilities for audiences and readers.

The question then becomes how to read *Macbeth*. For reading is active – not a passive absorption of a given body of meaning, but a collaboration between text and reader. Several of the essays printed here comment upon alternative ways of reading the play – which, once more, is not a stable, unitary edifice. This interpretive scope is apparent also in the way theatre directors have continuously reconstituted *Macbeth*, cutting, adding and supplying 'business'; this is necessary, they find, to make it 'work'. Graham Holderness (essay 12) shows how the play has been re-produced to diverse ends in the cinema. He considers which approaches may open the Shakespearean text to question, praising the Japanese film *Throne of Blood* precisely because it does not suggest the tragic inevitability that has often been found in *Macbeth*. Films may help us to liberate a radical potential in the play.

Holderness draws attention to the extent to which the re-production of Shakespeare is institutionalised – enmeshed with assumptions about cultural hierarchy in which commerce and the state (the education system, subsidised theatre) have a part. This is not new; in Shakespeare's time theatre was involved both in the market and in royal and noble patronage: the players took money at the door and were invited to perform at court. Cultural materialists try not to separate culture from the conditions of its production, noting how Shakespeare especially has become a cultural authority over which diverse interests may compete but which it is difficult to avoid.

Much of the authority of Shakespeare is transmitted through the education system (hence the present volume). *Educating Rita* also has become part of this system, and how this has happened is worth a glance partly for the light it casts on how institutions transmit and use Shakespeare and literature. Willy Russell's play was first pro-duced, in 1980, by the Royal Shakespeare Company. It was voted best comedy of the year in London and made into a film in 1983, but retained nevertheless an association with 'quality' culture, mainly because of its thoughtful treatment of ideas about literature. Hence, in part, its appearance on school syllabuses. The edition I found to buy, in a large bookshop near the university in Bristol, has been edited with this in view by Richard Adams, an English teacher in a mixed comprehensive school, for the 'Longman Study Texts' series in 1985; it had been reprinted eight times by 1988. As well as the play, this edition contains supporting materials for informed study: a 'personal essay' by Willy Russell explaining that Rita's experience was partly his own, an introduction on topics such as 'structure and characterization', notes, and 'study questions'. Although this sup-porting material in some ways encourages in the student Rita's independent attitude to literature, it also reasserts literature's author-ity. One of the study questions is: 'Have you ever been daunted by the prospect of reading and studying a classic by some major author, but derived immense enjoyment from the exercise once you have got into it?' And why not, indeed? – except that the phrasing, perhaps fearful that some students will be tempted to answer 'No!', predeter-mines some of the issues. Another question invites students to use their own words 'to convey as clearly as you can by illustration and argument the distinction between a tragic happening and true tragedy'.[17] We are not invited to ponder whether the distinction is satisfactory, or in whose interests it might be operating. Again, 'It was Shakespeare, I thought it was gonna be dead borin'', Rita exclaims, but the note hastens to reassure the student, in the guise of informing him or her, that this is 'England's greatest poet and dramatist: his works are read and studied, both in the original and in translation, all over the world'.[18] So the status of Shakespeare is reasserted at the very moment when Rita might bring it into question. The tendency of authority to reinscribe itself within texts that offer to comment upon it is repeated on the cover of this edition of *Educating Rita*, which shows some of the books Rita mentions – and on the top of the pile lies this very volume: it has joined the processes of literary education which it is in part re-evaluating.

Rita is a good play for reading in schools because it invites students to think about their own problems, or some of them, when they are 'doing English'. Frank comes to regret the loss of Rita's initial naïve response: 'to pass examinations', he says, 'you're going to have to suppress, perhaps even abandon your uniqueness'. He condemns even her admiration for his own poetry, because it requires a wide literary knowledge in order to recognise the allusions.[19] Literary criticism, the play shows, is an institution, a discourse whose language we may learn if we want to join in. Finding that Rita has progressed to the point where she does not need him, Frank expostulates bitterly: 'Found a better song to sing have you? No – you've found a different song, that's all – and on your lips it's shrill and hollow and tuneless.'[20] However, this is rather sentimental (Frank has become attached to Rita) – after all, Rita's untutored state produced her 'common-sense' sexist comment about Lady Macbeth being 'a cow'. Our 'innocent' understandings are also in fact social, they derive from the culture into which we have been socialised.

In learning the routines of literary criticism, then, Rita is adding competence in an additional discourse to the ones she has already, and, moreover, appreciates thereby that there is more than one way of seeing the world. So perhaps, as the play finally suggests, a person such as her gains an enhanced power to choose. This seems the kind of outcome one might hope for from an educational experience, but it would be a mistake to underestimate the structural inertia that impedes new kinds of understanding. Rita finds that her new awareness cuts her off from her family and friends: 'I'm a freak. I can't talk to the people I live with any more . . . I'm a half-caste.'[21]

Furthermore, it is doubtful whether Rita's freedom to choose will progress very far while conservative attitudes – in respect of literature, tragedy, gender, the individual and the political system – are maintained as the 'obvious' framework for the very discourse (literary criticism) that is supposed to open up new vistas. Individual students and teachers cannot just jump clear of the institutions of literary criticism, any more than a New Casebook can. Rita has difficulty opening the window in Frank's room: 'I'm not surprised, my dear', he says, 'It hasn't been opened for generations.'[22]

NOTES

1. Willy Russell, *Educating Rita*, ed. Richard Adams (London, 1985), pp. 39–40.

2. Ibid., pp. 40–1.

3. Ibid., p. 25.

4. Ibid., pp. 40–1.

5. Raymond Williams, *Modern Tragedy*, revised edn (London, 1979), pp. 46–7.

6. Ibid., p. 47.

7. Russell, *Educating Rita*, p. 19.

8. Ibid., p. 41.

9. See, for example, John Bayley, *Shakespeare and Tragedy* (London, 1981), pp. 164–6, 184.

10. Williams, *Modern Tragedy*, pp. 62–3.

11. Bertolt Brecht, *Plays Volume II* (London, 1962), p. 207.

12. On Bakhtin and carnival see Peter Stallybrass and Allon White, *The Politics and Poetics of Transgression* (London, 1986).

13. On the argument of this paragraph, see further in the present collection the essays by Stallybrass, Belsey, Evans, Sinfield, Dollimore and Holderness.

14. See Gary Taylor and Michael Warren (eds), *The Division of the Kingdoms: Shakespeare's two versions of 'King Lear'* (Oxford, 1986).

15. This remark, in respect of Forster's *Howards End* (Russell, *Educating Rita*, p. 19), is omitted from the film.

16. Don Wayne, 'New Historicism', in Martin Coyle, Peter Garside, Malcolm Kelsall and John Peck (eds), *Encyclopedia of Literature and Criticism* (London, 1990), p. 795.

17. Russell, *Educating Rita*, p. 91.

18. Ibid., pp. 39, 84.

19. Ibid., pp. 48, 67–8.

20. Ibid., p. 69.

21. Ibid., p. 45.

22. Ibid., p. 53.

1

'Macbeth' and Masculine Values

MARILYN FRENCH

There is an ambiguity about gender roles in *Macbeth* as there is in *King Lear*, but here it is the keynote of the play, the 'myth' from which everything else springs (as in *Lear*, the values implicit in the opening dialogue and the division of the kingdom are the 'myth'; and, as in *Othello*, the opening scene, with its clear contempt for 'feminine' values, provides the 'myth'). This ambiguity is embodied in the Witches who open the tragedy. Their chant, 'Fair is foul, and foul is fair', is a legend of moral and aesthetic ambiguity, but the Witches themselves incarnate ambiguity of gender. They are female, but have beards; they are aggressive and authoritative, but seem to have power only to create petty mischief. Their persons, their activities, and their song serve to link ambiguity about gender to moral ambiguity.

The reason ambiguity of gender is an element in the play is that Shakespeare did indeed associate certain qualities with the two genders. Perhaps he was shocked, and his imagination triggered by a passage in Holinshed describing women in Scotland fighting with hardiness, courage, and unshrinking bloodthirstiness.[1] But he makes Macbeth's Scotland a world of what seems to be constant war, that is, a 'heroic' culture. In such worlds, the felicities of life must be put aside, and procreation is tenuous: the means by which life is sustained become all important. His sense of such worlds is demonstrated in IV. iii, when Macduff tries to convince Malcolm to raise an army and oppose Macbeth. He tells Malcolm 'Each new morn / New

14

widows howl, new orphans cry'. Ross alludes to depredation of the feminine principle: Scotland 'cannot be called our mother, but our grave'. Malcolm's presence in the country, he says, 'would create new soldiers, make our women fight' (IV.iii.165–6, 178). In 'heroic' worlds, women must become as men, and the loss such a situation entails to the culture at large is the subject of the tragedy.

The world of Scotland is one of blood and brutality. Indeed, the first human words of the play are 'What bloody man is that?' The answer describes the hero, Macbeth:

> Disdaining Fortune, with his brandish'd steel,
> Which smok'd with bloody execution,
> Like valor's minion carv'd out his passage
> Till he fac'd the slave;
> Which nev'r shook hands, nor bade farewell to him,
> Till he unseam'd him from the nave to th' chops,
> And fix'd his head upon our battlements.
>
> (I.ii.17–23)

Such a description might shock and appal an audience, might imply that the hero is not totally admirable, if not for the fact that we hear only praise for Macbeth. He is 'brave Macbeth', 'valor's minion', 'valiant cousin', and 'worthy gentleman'. Most of the praise comes from Duncan, the King, the authority figure. The Sergeant's hideous description of the fighters' motivations: 'Except they meant to bathe in reeking wounds, / Or memorise another Golgotha, / I cannot tell', reaps only more praise and reward.

At the conclusion of this tragedy, we accept without demur the judgment that Macbeth is a butcher. In fact, however, he is no more a butcher at the end than he is at the beginning. Macbeth lives in a culture that values butchery. Throughout the play manhood is equated with the ability to kill. Power is the highest value in Scotland, and in Scottish culture, power is military prowess. Macbeth's crime is not that he is a murderer: he is praised and rewarded for being a murderer. His crime is a failure to make the distinction his culture expects among the objects of his slaughter.

A world that maintains itself by violence must, for the sake of sanity, fence off some segment – family, the block, the neighbourhood, the state – within which violence is not the proper mode of action. In this 'civilised' segment of the world, law, custom, hierarchy, and tradition are supposed to supersede the right of might. Although this inner circle is no more 'natural' or 'unnatural' than the outer one (so far as we can judge. Some people believe that aggression is profoundly 'natural' to humankind. I believe humans are basically timorous, and that aggression is forcibly taught, learned under duress. Neither position however can be proven), the play insists that the inner world is bound in accordance with a principle of nature which is equivalent to a divine law.

From the perspective of this study, the inner world is one which harmonises the two gender principles. Ruled by law, inherited legitimacy, hierarchy, and rights of ownership, the inner world also demands a degree of subordination in all its members. Everyone, including the ruler, must relinquish some worldly power (increasingly as one goes down the social scale) in favour of the good of the whole, if felicity and an environment favourable to procreation is to exist. Those with great power must restrain it; those without power must accept their places gracefully. Without such relinquishment, felicities like friendship, ceremony, orderly succession, peaceful love, hospitality, pleasure, and even the ability to sleep at night become difficult or impossible. An essential condition of this inviolable segment of the world is that the laws bind by themselves. They are not enforceable because enforcement is part of the larger outer sphere, the violent world. If the laws of the inner world must be enforced, that world becomes identical with the outer one. The laws therefore exist only in so far as the members of the group abide by them. Macbeth chooses to break the rules.

The factor responsible for Macbeth's doing so is Lady Macbeth. Although it is clear that Macbeth has, before the opening of the play, considered taking over the kingdom by force, it is also clear from his hesitation that he could easily be dissuaded from killing Duncan. And within the feminine/masculine polarity of morals and roles in Shakespeare's division of experience, it is Lady Macbeth's function so to dissuade him. But Lady Macbeth, a powerful person, is drawn to the role in which worldly power resides. She seems to be, by the world's standards, an exemplary wife. She encourages and supports her husband in good wifely fashion; she does not undermine him; she sees, knows, and understands the terms of the world she lives in, and she accepts them.

Yet at the end of the play, when her husband earns the attribute of 'butcher', she, who has not personally performed acts of violence, is called 'fiend-like'. In Shakespeare's eyes, Macbeth has violated moral law; Lady Macbeth has violated natural law. Her reasoning, in urging Macbeth to the murder, is not unlike that of Macdonwald: he is called *traitor* and *slave*. Both of these terms refer to the ethical world of legitimacy: one suggests resistance to the currently constituted authority; the other insists on illegitimacy. But Lady Macbeth is not so judged; she is seen as supernaturally evil. Her crime is heinous because it violates her social role, which has been erected into a principle of experience: she fails to uphold the feminine principle. For her, as for Goneril, this failure plunges her more deeply into a pit of evil than any man can ever fall.

The imagery of the play is divided into masculine and feminine categories. Blood and royal robes, symbolic of male prowess, authority, and legitimacy, are opposed to procreative and nourishing images of babies, children, the female breast, and milk. Lady Macbeth informs us of her values at her first appearance: Macbeth, she says, is flawed by being 'too full o' th' milk of human kindness' (I.v.17). Laid against the view of Macbeth the warrior that we have just been given, this is an astonishing perception. It has less to do with Macbeth, however, than with his lady. She who, in Shakespeare's view, should properly encourage this milky side of her husband, resolves instead to align herself with the male principle, in a passage explicitly connecting gender to role and moral value:

> Come, you spirits
> That tend on mortal thoughts, unsex me here,
> And fill me from the crown to the toe topfull
> Of direst cruelty! . . . Come to my woman's breasts,
> And take my milk for gall.
>
> (I.v.40–8)

In her conversation with Macbeth (I. vii), she argues from a perspective that equates manliness with killing. Macbeth protests: 'I dare do all that may become a man; / Who dares do more is none.' She insists: 'When you durst do it, then you were a man; / And to be more than what you were, you would / Be so much more the man.' The 'it' in question is killing; and manliness, for Lady Macbeth, clearly *excludes* compassion and nurturing:

> I have given suck, and know
> How tender 'tis to love the babe that milks me;
> I would, while it was smiling in my face,
> Have pluck'd my nipple from his boneless gums,
> And dash'd the brains out, had I so sworn as you
> Have done to this.
>
> (I.vii.54–9)

Both agree that manliness is the highest standard of behaviour: what they argue about is what the term comprehends. Macbeth's real problem is that he cannot articulate, even to himself, what is wrong with his wife's logic. He floats in vague dread, a sense of wrongness that seems to him to reverberate to the heavens (although his dread is not specifically Christian or religious – he jumps the life to come with ease), but the values he is obliquely conscious of as being in some impalpable way significant have no currency and therefore no vocabulary in his culture. At the end of their conversation, he accepts his wife's definition of manliness; it is, after all, identical to that of his – and her – culture as a whole.

> Bring forth men-children only!
> For thy undaunted mettle should compose
> Nothing but males.
>
> (I.vii.72–4)

Still, he continues to feel uneasy, and Lady Macbeth, gazing down at the sleeping Duncan, has an intimation that there is something unpleasant about killing a father. Their trepidations heighten our sense that the inner circle, the place where murder is illegitimate, is indeed sacred.

And once the deed is done, Shakespeare suggests that the entire character of the world is changed. When the texture of the inner circle is identical to that of the outer one, the connection between means and ends is broken. Instead of procreation and felicity, the end of power becomes more power alone, consolidation and extension of power: thus, life becomes hell. The porter announces the change, knowing he is in hell even though the place is too cold for it.

In Scotland, the feminine has taken to wearing beards and acting aggressively. Lady Macbeth's renunciation of her role leads to the murder of a king, father, guest. These actions lead to a new ambience, a world in which the feminine principle is being wiped out. That this is a 'natural' calamity is suggested by the 'unnatural' events that follow: an attack on a female falcon by a 'mousing owl'; Duncan's horses 'contending 'gainst obedience' and eating each other. Confusion in human gender roles leads in this play to confusion in the hierarchies of nature, as well as to the destruction of one gender principle – Malcolm and Donalbain flee a kingdom where 'there's no mercy left' (II.iii.146). Duncan's murder is called a 'breach in nature' (II.iii.113). [And] the consequences of Duncan's murder involve the destruction of particularly women and children. . . .

Dame Helen Gardner ties this slaughter to its larger field. She sees Macbeth's anxiety before the murder of Duncan as a fear 'not that he will be cut down by Macduff, but that having murdered his own humanity he will enter a world of appalling loneliness, of meaningless activity, unloved himself and unable to love. . . . It is not terror of heaven's vengeance that makes him pause, but the terror of moral isolation.'[2] Having killed his own ends, Macbeth inexorably kills them for others, with the same dogged and mindless tenacity that Don John and Iago show.

The victory of the masculine principle over the feminine is a victory of means over ends, and is an empty victory as a result. The severing of connection between means and ends has consequences for the 'victors' as well as for the victims. And it is this that is ideologically important and unusual about *Macbeth*. The Thane and his wife both know there is none can call their power to account. In a world of power, linear reason, and control, there is no reason *not* to kill Duncan. The King has set the succession elsewhere, although it is Macbeth's arm that holds the country up. Lady Macbeth sees this very clearly. Macbeth, however, dreads the consequences he may unleash. 'If it were done when 'tis done' it would be well, but 'bloody instructions' are lessons to others, and boomerang. Beyond that, there are vague reasons for fear.

Macbeth's fears are justified. For with the eradication of pity, compassion, and 'masculine' codes aimed at 'feminine' ends, the felicities that make Macbeth's life worthwhile vanish. When home becomes part of the war zone, life is merely battle. Macbeth's hypocritical lament over the dead Duncan is ironically prophetic:

> Had I but died an hour before this chance,
> I had liv'd a blessed time; for from this instant
> There's nothing serious in mortality:
> All is but toys: renown and grace is dead,
> The wine of life is drawn, and the mere lees
> Is left this vault to brag of.
>
> (II.iii.95–100)

There is another irony in the play. Duncan is almost always seen as saintly: the epithet 'gracious' is continually applied to him. He combines 'masculine' authority with 'feminine' meekness, concern with himself with concern for the whole. He is nutritive: he tells Macbeth 'I have begun to plant thee, and will labour / To make thee full of growing' (I.iv.28–9). He combines the gender principles; he incarnates harmonious unity. When Macbeth considers the violation the murder of such a man would be, he uses masculine and feminine images:

> And pity, like a naked new-born babe,
> Striding the blast, or heaven's cherubim, hors'd
> Upon the sightless couriers of the air,
> Shall blow the horrid deed in every eye,
> That tears shall drown the wind.
>
> (I.vii.21–5)

Nevertheless, Duncan participates in the unequal value system of his culture. His grateful approval of the hideous slaughter performed in battle, a slaughter designed after all to ensure *his* continued supremacy, bathes him as well as Macbeth and the other warriors in the blood of 'reeking wounds'. Like Macbeth, Duncan is destroyed by the principle to which he grants priority.

The scenes following his murder swiftly and sharply depict a world gone insane from lack of balance. Murder follows murder until the entire country is a death camp. And the terms used by the characters remain sickeningly the same. Macbeth eggs on the hired murderers with the same challenge his wife threw to him.

> **First Murderer**   We are men, my liege.
> **Macbeth**   Ay, in the catalogue ye go for men.
>
> (III.i.90–1)

True men, he claims, would murder an enemy. And so they prove themselves.

During the scene in which Macbeth is terrified by Banquo's ghost, Lady Macbeth several times turns on her husband contemptuously: 'Are you a man?' (III.iv.57). He is, she says, 'quite unmann'd in folly' (III.iv.72), and scornfully describes his terror as more suitable to 'a woman's story at a winter's fire, / Authoris'd by her grandam' (III.iv.64–5). Macbeth insists 'What man dare, I dare', and argues that only if he were to tremble facing a real enemy could he be called 'the baby of a girl'. When the ghost vanishes, he sighs 'I am a man again' (III.iv.98, 105).

In worlds dominated by the masculine principle, the feminine principle is partly scorned, but it is also partly feared. It is, after all, the pole of nature and feeling; it is uncontrollable in its spontaneity and its disregard for power. And most important, as the pole of procreation, it embraces the future. Thus, although Fleance is not logically a threat to Macbeth, it is the child Fleance whom the childless King fears. Why should a childless man worry about who will inherit the kingdom? Macbeth's anxiety is psychologically profound: he flails wildly, trying to secure the ends for which power is supposed to exist – which for him at this point have shrunk to the ability to sleep at night.

The very existence of Fleance prevents Macbeth from feeling secure. Moreover in the Witches' evocations for the tormented King, two infants are central. Cleanth Brooks finds the babe to be 'perhaps the most powerful symbol in the tragedy'.[3] The first baby to appear is bloody, symbolising Macduff, who, born 'unnaturally' – covered with blood from his mother's caesarian delivery – will perform the ritual act of killing the tyrant. (The implications of this are opaque to me. Perhaps Macduff, not being 'tainted' by having arrived in the world through the female vagina, is 'pure' in a special way, and able to destroy the tyrant. Or perhaps, having been born bloody, he has an imperviousness to certain fears, or a lack of certain delicacies, which make him able to defeat Scotland's greatest warrior. The implications of the vision are not essential to the play, but they are to the 'myth' underlying the play.)

The second babe in the vision is clean, born naturally; he is crowned and bears a tree, which may suggest the coming of Birnam Wood to Dunsinane, but more significantly suggests a 'natural' and organic line of succession – all the way to James I of England.

The play reaches its moral climax in IV.ii, with the attack on Lady Macduff and the murder of her child onstage. This horrifying scene is emblematic of the character of a world in which ends have been devalued. The horror and the pity it arouses in the audience are morally exemplary: this is what happens, what it feels like to live in a world in which power can no longer distinguish the elements it was designed to protect. But the moral climax of the play is also its moral turning point.

The next scene shows Macduff, ignorant of what has happened to his family, describing to Malcolm the scene in Scotland. G. Wilson Knight comments on Lady Macduff's claim that her husband's flight was caused by fear rather than love or wisdom, 'It is partly true. . . . Macduff is forced to sacrifice the bond of family love'. Wilbur Sanders points out that in his discussion with Malcolm, Macduff actually condones the prostitution of his countrywomen.[4] It is in this scene, too, that the images of Scotland as grave rather than mother, and of women fighting, occur. It is in this scene that the real battle lines of the play are drawn. But the winning streak of the one 'side' of things is broken when Macduff hears the news about his family. 'Dispute it like a man' (IV.iii.220), Malcolm urges, using the same language we have heard before.

And Macduff, for the first time in the play, expands the meaning of the word *man*: 'But I must also feel it as a man', he says, recalling the blind Gloucester, who without eyes sees how the world goes, sees it 'feelingly'. Macduff refuses either to cry or to bluster: 'O I could play the woman with mine eyes, / And braggart with my tongue' (IV.iii.230–1). He agrees finally to curtail his mourning, to Malcolm's satisfaction: 'This tune goes manly'.

Thus, the opening scene of the denouement, despite Macduff's definition of a man as one who feels, is still dominated by the same terms in which the play opened. And the play ends as it began, in a totally masculine world. Courage, prowess, the ability to kill, and compassion, nurturance, and mercy, are not equally valuable qualities to be held in a flexible balance. Priority continues to be given to the first set. Siward's son, for instance, who 'only lived but till he was a man', is killed in his first battle. Ross tells old Siward that 'like a man he died'. The old man should have been played by John Wayne. He has only one question: did his son die fighting or fleeing?: 'Had he his hurts before?' (V.ix.12). This time it is Malcolm who raises a minority voice: 'He's worth more sorrow, / And that I'll spend for him'. The implication of this remark, plus the different tone of the dialogue at the close of this battle – saddened, heavy – compared to that of the triumphant dialogue at the close of the battle scene that opens the play, suggests that feeling will be at least an item in the new governance of Scotland.

But it will still occupy a secondary – or even lower – place. In the dialogue with Malcolm, it is Siward who has the last word: 'He's worth no more'. His mother might not agree. In this world, sons exist to go to war, and women exist to give birth to sons who are born to kill or be killed in battle. The language remains the same right to the end of the play. Macduff's statement to Macbeth that he was not born of woman makes Macbeth as 'effeminate' as Juliet makes Romeo: he tells Macduff the announcement has '*cow'd* my better part of man' (V.vii.18) (italics mine). And the play concludes with Macduff's entrance bearing the bloody severed head of the butcher in his bloody hands, and his triumphal, 'Hail, King!'

So, although some balance is restored to the kingdom, there is no change in its value structure. What is restored is the sacred inner circle, in which men are expected to refrain from applying the standards of the outer one: what is reasserted is moral schizophrenia.

Such a division may have seemed inescapable to Shakespeare. The world is continually threatened with violence and aggression; indeed, it is (either) because of this that the world grants priority to the masculine principle (or) because the world grants priority to the masculine principle that this happens. In any case, Shakespeare clearly saw the danger to society of such a priority; he examines the cost of allowing power, might, to override every other value. His conclusions are far more profound than some pious or conventional readers will allow.

It is sometimes stated, for instance, that Macbeth kills because of the 'passion' of ambition, which is permitted to overcome his 'reason'. He kills, it is said, 'order and degree': since it is a critical truism that order and degree are good, that passion is evil and reason good, it is clear Macbeth is evil. We hardly need critics to give us this information. A more sympathetic and probing critic has stated that Lady Macbeth denies the existence of 'irrational values' and thus is destroyed by them.[5] But some readers have commented that Macbeth's death is an anticlimax, that he is already dead in the spirit before Macduff meets him.[6] His 'Tomorrow and tomorrow and tomorrow' speech allows no other conclusion.

If passion means emotion, feeling, it is Macbeth's 'passion', in so far as we see it, that makes him dread the murder. He does not kill out of passion, but out of reason. He and his wife have considered the entire political situation, and know that he has the power to seize control. They are correct in their judgment. They are what people today who admire such thinking call 'hardheaded'. What they forget, what Macbeth only intimates, what Heilman suggests by mentioning 'irrational values', is that political considerations are not the only ones that matter. The wholeness of life matters, although humans are given to forget that. And the only rationality that is of benefit to humans is one that is aware of all of the qualities of life.

What happens to Macbeth, long before the final battle, is that he loses all reason for living. He has cut himself off from everything that makes life worth living: 'honour, love, obedience, troops of friends', all life's felicities. Despite the love shown between them in the early scenes, his wife's death barely touches Macbeth. She gave up her part in his life when she renounced the gender principle she was responsible for.

Shakespeare sets the feminine principle, those values to which

Judaeo-Christian culture has always given lip service and little real respect, and which Christianity projects into an afterlife, firmly within the mortal span, within everyday experience. We may not repudiate the qualities associated with pleasure and procreation, with nature and giving up of control, without injuring ourselves, perhaps even maiming or destroying ourselves. It is hardly the life to come that we breach: it is life here.

From Marilyn French, *Shakespeare's Division of Experience* (London, 1982), pp. 242–51.

NOTES

[In this extract from her book *Shakespeare's Division of Experience* Marilyn French identifies the world of the play as masculine and founded in violence – Duncan's, Macduff's and Malcolm's, as well as Macbeth's. Lady Macbeth seems evil because she does not uphold a countervailing 'feminine principle'. French has been criticised for attributing such a sharp gender division to Shakespeare, but nevertheless she offers a notable feminist re-vision of values in *Macbeth*. The original notes relating her account to those of earlier critics have been abbreviated. *Macbeth* is quoted from *The Riverside Shakespeare*, ed. G. B. Evans (Boston and London, 1974). Ed.]

1. Raphael Holinshed, 'The Description of Scotland', prefaced to *The Historie of Scotland* (London, 1585), p. 21.

2. Helen Gardner, *The Business of Criticism* (Oxford, 1959), p. 61.

3. Cleanth Brooks, *The Well-Wrought Urn* (London, 1968), p. 31.

4. G. Wilson Knight, *The Imperial Theme* (London, 1931), p. 142; Wilbur Sanders, *The Dramatist and the Received Idea* (Cambridge, 1968), p. 262.

5. Robert Heilman, 'The Lear World', *English Institute Essays: 1948*, ed. D. A. Robertson, Jr (New York, 1949), p. 53.

6. Notably Gardner, *Business of Criticism*, p. 61, and L. C. Knights, *Some Shakespearean Themes* (London, 1959), p. 15.

2

'Macbeth' and Witchcraft

PETER STALLYBRASS

For students of *Macbeth*, witchcraft has always presented a problem. At the one extreme, we have scholars like T. A. Spalding and W. C. Curry who have unearthed some of the historical *minutiae* of medieval and Renaissance concepts of witchcraft;[1] at the other extreme, we have critics who accept the play's witchcraft only as a form of psychological symbolism. Since the publications of Keith Thomas's *Religion and the Decline of Magic* (1971) and Alan Macfarlane's *Witchcraft in Tudor and Stuart England* (1970), the latter position has seemed less tenable. But this does not mean that we should return to the (admittedly useful) positivistic data-gathering of Spalding and Curry to understand the function of witchcraft in *Macbeth*. I see little point, for instance, in attempting to *classify* the Weird Sisters as witches or warlocks or norns (distinctions which were rarely observed by Tudor and Stuart witchcraft treatises or reports of trials). Such classifications tend to emphasise the exoticism of witchcraft beliefs without beginning to explain how such beliefs could ever have been held.

It is, indeed, worth emphasising the 'normality' of witchcraft beliefs. Although witchcraft accusations reached epidemic proportions in sixteenth- and seventeenth-century Europe, witchcraft beliefs are endemic in many societies. Their frequency, however, should not be taken as evidence for the truth of witchcraft (there is no proof, for instance, that 'witches' eat their own children, cause sickness, plague or famine, or have sexual relations with devils) but as evidence of the social utility of such beliefs in a variety of societies. An adequate explanation of witchcraft, then, needs to have a double focus: on the one hand, it must describe the actual beliefs and explain how they fit within a particular cosmology; on the other hand, it must take into account the *function* of such beliefs ('a myth provides a charter for action').[2]

Witchcraft beliefs are one way of asserting distinctions; they 'sharpen definitions',[3] as Mary Douglas puts it, including definitions of political and familial roles. They can be used, for instance, to account for the 'unnatural' ambition of a rival or for the 'unnatural' power of a woman. In doing so, such beliefs imply and legitimate their opposite, the 'natural'. In short, witchcraft beliefs are less a reflection of a real 'evil' than a social construction from which we learn more about the accuser than the accused, more about the social institutions which tolerate/encourage/act on those accusations than about the activities of those people (in England, mainly women, mainly poor) who were prosecuted as witches. What Mary Douglas says of dirt could be said of witchcraft: it 'is never a unique, isolated event' but rather 'the by-product of a systematic ordering and classification . . . in so far as ordering involves rejecting inappropriate elements'.[4] Witchcraft accusations are a way of reaffirming a particular order against outsiders, or of attacking an internal rival, or of attacking 'deviance'. Witchcraft in *Macbeth*, I will maintain, is not simply a reflection of a pre-given order of things: rather, it is a particular working upon, and legitimation of, the hegemony of patriarchy.

WITCHCRAFT AND MONARCHY

The English government had, at least since 1300, been concerned with 'witches' – 'with sorcerers, because they might attempt to kill the king, with prophets (including astrologers) because they might forecast the hour of his death'. The Duke of Buckingham, accused of treason in 1521, had been encouraged by a prophecy that he would be king, although he had been warned that the prophet, a Carthusian monk, 'might be deceived by the devil'. In 1558, Sir Anthony Fortescue was arrested for sorcery, having cast a horoscope which stated that the Queen 'should not live passing the next spring', and in 1580, Nicholas Johnson was accused of 'making her Majesty's picture in wax'.[5] This last case was one of the factors in the passing of a new Act in 1580–1 which attacked the 'divers persons wickedly disposed' who had 'not only wished her Majesty's death, but also by divers means practised and sought to know how long her Highness should live, and who should reign after her decease, and what changes and alterations should thereby happen.'[6] The Act went on to attack all those who, 'by any prophecying, witchcraft, conjurations or other like unlawfull means whatsoever', attempted to harm the monarch or to meddle in her affairs. In England, then, there was already a clear connection between prophecy, witchcraft, and monarchy before James ascended the throne.

In Scotland, James was making his own connections. There is little evidence that he had an interest in witchcraft before 1590, but the sensational trials of that year changed his attitude. More than 300 witches were alleged to have met and confessions were extorted, with the aid of torture, which pointed to a conspiracy directed by the Earl of Bothwell against the king himself. James took an active part in the trial, and Agnes Samson's report of 'the very words which passed between the King's Majesty and his Queen at Oslo in Norway the first night of their marriage' made him give 'more credit to the rest'.[7]

But if the trial triggered James's interest in witchcraft, we may suggest two possible determinants of the actual form his interest took. The first is, paradoxical though it may seem, his very desire to be in the intellectual vanguard. We need to remember that the witch craze was not the last fling of residual medieval 'superstition', but, at least in part, the potent construction of some of the foremost intellectuals of the time, including Bodin. It may well be, as Christine Larner has suggested,[8] that it was James's attempt to keep up with intellectual developments on the Continent after his contact with scholars in Denmark in 1589 which first aroused his interest in witchcraft.

But if his interest was stimulated by Continental ideas, his new belief consolidated his pre-existing interest in the theory and practice of godly rule. If the King was God's representative on earth, then who could be a more likely victim of the devil's arts than he? In his early work on the Book of Revelations, James had associated the devil with Antichrist, in his guise of the Pope, but it was not difficult to imagine that the devil employed more than one agency. To suggest, then, that the monarchy was under demonic attack was to glorify the institution of monarchy, since that implied that it was one of the bastions protecting this world from the triumph of Satan. As Stuart Clark says, 'demonism was, logically speaking, one of the presuppositions of the metaphysics of order on which James's political ideas ultimately rested.' Clark also shows how this kind of *antithetical* thinking is the logical corollary of *analogical* thinking. If kingship is legitimated by analogy to God's rule over the earth, and the father's rule over the family and the head's rule over the body, witchcraft establishes the opposite analogies, whereby the Devil attempts to rule over the earth, and the woman over the family, and the body over the head.[9] ...

'MACBETH' AND HOLINSHED

If it was the accession of James to the English throne which suggested a play about Scottish history, and about James's own ancestry in particular, it is worth noting how Shakespeare utilised Holinshed, his main source for the play. To begin with, he simplified the outlines of the story to create a structure of clear antitheses. Holinshed's Duncan is a weak king, 'negligent ... in punishing offenders',[10] and unable to control the kingdom, whereas Shakespeare's Duncan is, as even Macbeth admits, 'clear in his great office' (I.vii.18). Holinshed's Macbeth has a legal right to the throne, since 'by the old lawes of the realme, the ordnance was, that if he that should succeed were not of able age to take the charge upon himselfe, he that was next of bloud unto him should be admitted', whereas Shakespeare makes little of Macbeth's claim. Moreover, Shakespeare omits any reference to the 'ten yeares in equall justice' during which Holinshed's Macbeth ruled after 'the feeble and slouthfull administration of Duncane' (Holinshed, pp. 172–3). Finally, Holinshed's Banquo is a party to Macbeth's plot to murder Duncan, whereas Shakespeare's Banquo is not.

What is striking about all these changes is that they transform dialectic into antithesis. Whereas Shakespeare's second historical tetralogy undoubtedly raises dialectical questions about sovereignty, *Macbeth* takes material eminently suitable for dialectical development (the weak ruler being overthrown by a ruler who establishes 'equall justice') and shapes it into a structural antithesis. One reason for the shaping of the sources in this way was, no doubt, royal patronage. This meant, for instance, that Banquo, James's ancestor, had to be shown in a favourable light, and it may be that James's views on godly rule and on 'the trew difference betwixt a lawfull, good King and an usurping Tyrant' were taken into account. Certainly, *Macbeth* differentiates as clearly as James's *Basilikon Doron* between the good king whose 'greatest suretie' is his people's good will and the tyrant who builds 'his suretie upon his peoples miserie'.[11]

Holinshed's account, though, suggested another factor by which the tyrant might be distinguished from the godly ruler: his relation to witchcraft. For Holinshed describes how Macbeth 'had learned of certaine wizzards' and had gained (false) confidence from a witch who told him 'that he should never be slaine with man born of anie woman' (Holinshed, p. 175). But even over the issue of witchcraft, Holinshed is not entirely clear, because the crucial prophecies which embolden his Macbeth are made by 'three women in strange and wild apparell, resembling creatures of elder world', and these women are later described as 'either the weird sisters, that is (as ye would say) the goddesses of destinie, or else some nymphs or feiries, indued with knowledge of prophesie by their necromenticall science' (Holinshed, pp. 171–2). It was probably these three women whom Dr Gwin transformed into the *Tres Sibyllae* who hailed James as King of Scotland and England in a performance presented to the king at Oxford on 27 August 1605.[12]

But for the Witches in *Macbeth* to have been presented as godly sibylls would have weakened the antithetical structure of the play. Only by making his Sisters forces of darkness could Shakespeare suggest demonic opposition to godly rule. And here Shakespeare had to supplement Holinshed's account of Macbeth. For although the political effects of usurpation are suggested by Holinshed's account of how, after Macbeth murdered Banquo, 'everie man began to doubt his owne life' (Holinshed, p. 174), there is little sense of the natural holocaust which Bolton saw as the logical outcome of the overthrow of sovereignty. For an image of a king's murder and the consequent turning of a country into 'a very hell upon earth', Shakespeare had to turn back to Holinshed's account of Donwald's murder of King Duff, a murder which is itself the consequence of the King's execution of Donwald's kinsmen for conspiring with witches against him. Many of the horrifying events which follow Duff's death (the darkening of the sun, lightning and tempests, cannibalism amongst animals) reappear, more or less transformed, in *Macbeth*, reaffirming through antithesis the order which has been overthrown – the order of monarchy, of patriarchy, of the head, of 'reason'.

THE WITCHES

'For Rebellion is as the sin of witchcraft' (I Samuel XV.23). And the first two scenes of *Macbeth* present both witches and rebellion. But what kind of witches are they? In the first scene, we can note several aspects of them: they are connected with disorder in nature (not only

thunder and lightning but also 'fog and filthy air'); they are associated with familiars (Graymalkin and Paddock), the common com-
panions of English witches but rarely mentioned in Scottish or
Continental prosecutions; they can 'hover'; they reverse moral values
('Fair is foul, and foul is fair' (I.i.10)); they presumably foresee the
future, since the third witch knows that the battle will be over by
sunset. The third scene, though, shows more clearly what seems to be
an ambiguity in the presentation of the Witches. On the one hand,
they have features typical of the English village 'witch', being old
women, 'wither'd' and with 'choppy fingers' and 'skinny lips'.
(Reginald Scot described English 'witches' as 'commonly old, lame,
bleare-eied, pale, fowle, and full of wrinkles'.)[13] Moreover, the
second witch kills swine and the first witch pursues a petty vendetta,
typical offences in English witch prosecutions. But, on the other
hand, they are mysterious and 'look not like th' inhabitants o' th'
earth' (I.iii.41), and they prophesy the future.

What is the function of this ambiguity? At one level, no doubt, it
enabled Shakespeare to draw upon the common belief in an 'evil' at
work in the English countryside whilst never reducing the play's
witches to village widows. But it was also structurally convenient
because it established a double perspective on evil, allowing for the
simultaneous sense of reduction in Macbeth as he becomes increasingly dependent on the 'midnight hags' (IV.i.47) and of his aspiration
as, after 'Disdaining Fortune' (I.ii.17) in the battle, he attempts to
grab hold of Providence itself. The double perspective operates
throughout the play. On the one hand, Macbeth is reduced to the
image of 'a dwarfish thief' (V.ii.22) before being literally reduced to
the head which Macduff carries onto the stage. At this level, evil is
conceptualised as eating up itself until nothing is left. But the
conceptualisation leaves no role for militant 'good' (and therefore
would not require the 'great revenge' (IV.iii.214) of Malcolm and
Macduff), and so the world of self-consuming evil is combined with a
dualistic world in which both the Witches and Macbeth threaten to
bring the world back to its first chaos or, as Bolton puts it, to create
'a very hell upon earth', the hell of a world without sovereignty.

LADY MACBETH, THE WITCHES, AND FAMILY STRUCTURE

The Witches open the play, but they appear in only the first and third scenes of the first Act. In the fifth and seventh scenes, the 'temptress' is Lady Macbeth. In other words, scenes in which female figures champion evil alternate with public scenes (Duncan and news of the battle in scene 2; the honouring of Macbeth, Banquo, and Malcolm in scene 4; Duncan's reception at Macbeth's castle in scene 6). And the public scenes, with the exception of the last, are exclusively male. If this foregrounds the female figures, Lady Macbeth is also equated with the Witches in more specific ways. As Mark Rose says, 'the third scene opens with the Witches alone, after which Macbeth enters and they hail him by his various titles. The fifth scene opens with Lady Macbeth alone, practising witchcraft. . . . And when Macbeth enters she, too, hails him by his titles.'[14] Moreover, Lady Macbeth and the Witches are equated by their equivocal relation to an implied norm of femininity. Of the Witches, Banquo says:

> You should be women,
> And yet your beards forbid me to interpret
> That you are so.
>   (I.iii.45–7)

And Lady Macbeth invokes the 'murd'ring ministers' (I.v.45) to unsex her.

The enticement of Macbeth both by the Witches and by his wife is briefly suggested in Holinshed's account of Macbeth, and in Holinshed's earlier account of Donwald's wife Shakespeare found a much expanded role given to a murderer's wife. But in neither account is any connection made between witchcraft and the murderer's wife. Again, we see the antithetical mode being strengthened in *Macbeth* by the development of analogies between 'perverted femininity', witchcraft, and a world turned upside down. The analogy was not, of course, new, and it is notoriously enshrined in *Malleus Maleficarum* where *Femina* is derived from *Fe* and *Minus* 'since [woman] is ever weaker to hold and preserve the faith.'[15]

But it is important to note the shift of emphasis when Lady Macbeth 'replaces' the witches. By this movement from the already damned to the secular world, the implications of the rejection of 'womanhood' are made explicit. Whereas the witches are difficult to categorise at all within the implied norm, in I.v Lady Macbeth is shown in the very attempt of overthrowing a norm inscribed in her own body. 'Remorse', 'compunctious visitings of Nature', and the 'milk' of 'woman's breasts' (I.v.41–5) are established as the 'feminine' virtues even as Lady Macbeth negates them. Indeed, because of the inscription of those virtues in Lady Macbeth, her relation to witch-craft is not as clear at the psychological as it is at the structural level. Although Lady Macbeth might say, like Joan la Pucelle, 'I exceed my sex' (*1 Henry VI*, I.ii.90), her relation to witchcraft is never as explicit as Joan's. For Joan is not merely *accused* of being a 'witch' and 'damned sorceress' (III.ii.38); her conjurings lead to the actual appearance of fiends upon the stage.

Nevertheless, Lady Macbeth's invocation of the 'murd'ring minis-ters' (I.v.45) as her children has particular resonance within the context of witchcraft, even if her ministers never appear. For her proclaimed role as mother/lover of the spirits implicitly subverts patriarchal authority in a manner typically connected with witch-craft. If the first Witch plans to come between a sailor and his wife in I.iii, Lady Macbeth herself breaks the bond with her husband by suggesting both his metaphysical and physical impotence (he is not 'a man' (I.vii.49)) because he is unworthy of the respect due to a patriarch, because he is 'a coward' (I.vii.43), and, possibly, because, as we learn later, his is 'a barren sceptre' (III.i.61). It is particularly ironic, then, that Macbeth says 'Bring forth men-children only' (I.vii.72). For the structural antitheses which the first act develops establish the relation between women, witchcraft, the undermining of patriarchal authority and sterility.

But how can the family be conceptualised if women are, literally, faithless? One way is to show that not all womanhood falls under the curse of witchcraft, and this is surely an important reason for the introduction of Lady Macduff in IV.ii, a scene which has no base in Holinshed. Indeed, it is the destruction of this 'ideal' family which leads to Macduff's revenge and the final denouement. But Lady Macduff is introduced late in the play, and we have already been presented with another way out of the dilemma: a family without women – Duncan and his sons, Malcolm and Donalbain, Banquo and his son Fleance (at the end of the play, Siward and his son Young Siward). On the one hand, there are the (virtuous) families of men; on the other hand, there are the antifamilies of women. And here, the notorious question, 'How many children had Lady Macbeth?' is not entirely irrelevant. For although Lady Macbeth says, 'I have given suck' (I.vii.54), her children are never seen on the stage, unlike the children of Duncan, Banquo, Macduff, and Siward. Are we not asked to accept a logical contradiction for the sake of a symbolic unity: Lady Macbeth is *both* an unnatural mother *and* sterile? This links her to the unholy family of the Witches, with their familiars and their brew which includes 'Finger of birth-strangled babe' and the blood of a sow which has eaten its own litter (IV.i.30 and 64–5). Like the Witches, Lady Macbeth and her husband constitute an 'unholy' family, a family whose only children are the 'murd'ring ministers'.

THE DEVELOPMENT OF LADY MACBETH AND THE WITCHES

I have been writing mainly of the ways in which the Witches and Lady Macbeth function in the first Act. But their functions are not constant throughout the play. Lady Macbeth is beginning to be developed into her own antithesis even before the murder takes place. 'Nature' is reasserted through her in its most compelling guise – the Law of the Father which, in this society, founds and is founded by the Law of the King. Thus, Lady Macbeth says that she would have murdered Duncan herself 'Had he not resembled / My father as he slept' (II.ii.12–13). And in the last act, she is transformed from the pitiless instigator to murder to the guilt-ridden sleep-walker whose thoughts return to 'the old man' who had 'so much blood in him' (V.i.38). Curry interprets her sleep-walking as 'demoniacal somnambulism'.[16] But surely this is to miss the dramatic point, which is the reassertion of 'the compunctious visitations of Nature' if only in sleep. Lady Macbeth's last words, indeed, are not of her own guilt but of the solicitous wife's care for her husband: 'give me your hand. . . . To bed, to bed, to bed' (V.i.64–6). But the transformation of Lady Macbeth is used to affirm developmentally the antithetical structure. It operates as a specific closure of discourse within the binary opposition of virago (witch)/wife.

If Lady Macbeth's changing function is marked by psychological change, the Witches' changing function is marked by the changing function of their prophecies. Much has been made of the fact that the Witches speak equivocally, that they are, as Macbeth says, 'imperfect speakers' (I.iii.70). But the apparitions of the fourth act are progressively *less* equivocal, moving from the 'armed head' to the 'bloody child' to the 'child crowned' to the 'show of eight kings, the last with a glass in his hand' which shows Banquo's descendants stretched out 'to th' crack of doom' (IV.i.117). The Witches here, far from being 'imperfect speakers', conjure up a vision whose truth is established by the presence of Banquo's descendant, James I. In this prophecy of the 'good', dramatic fate (as yet incomplete) joins hands with completed political fate.

As with Lady Macbeth, then, so with the Witches: they are constructed so as to manifest their own antithesis. Cursed witches prophesy the triumph of godly rule. At one level, no doubt, this implies that even evil works providentially. As James himself had declared in the preface to his *Daemonologie* (1597):

> For where the devilles intention in them is ever to perish, either the soule or the body, or both of them, that he is so permitted to deale with: God by the contrarie, drawes ever out of that evill glorie to himselfe.
>
> (Sig. A4)

But at another level, the association of the Witches with the workings of Providence is part of the process by which attention is focused upon Macbeth alone. In I.i, the Witches are invoked by their familiars; in I.v, Lady Macbeth invokes the spirits. But, in the third act, it is Macbeth, who had to be 'invoked' to do the deed, who invokes the night to 'Scarf up the tender eye of pitiful Day' (III.ii.47). But Macbeth's conjunctions made even

> though the treasure
> Of nature's germens tumble all together,
> Even till destruction sicken
> (IV.i.58–60)

lead to a future in which he, with his 'fruitless crown' (III.i.60), has no place. At the end, his only 'familiar' is 'Direness, familiar to my slaughterous thoughts' (V.v.14). ...

Witchcraft, prophecy and magic function in *Macbeth* as ways of developing a particular conceptualisation of social and political order. Witchcraft is associated with female rule and the overthrowing of patriarchal authority which in turn leads to the 'womanish' (both cowardly and instigated by women) killing of Duncan, the 'holy' father who establishes both family and state. This in turn leads to the reversals in the cosmic order which the Old Man and Ross describe, and to the reversals in the patriarchal order, culminating in the killing of Lady Macduff and her son. The conclusion of the play re-establishes both the offended (and offending?) father, a father, paradoxically, 'not born of woman' (V.iii.4) (does this imply that he is unnatural or untainted?), and the offended son/king. And the Witches can simply disappear, their evil supplanted by the prophetic vision of Banquo's line and by the 'heavenly gift of prophecy' and 'miraculous work' (IV.iii.157 and 147) of a legitimate king.

CONCLUSION

This aspect of *Macbeth* as a work of cultural 'ordering' could, of course, only make claims to 'truth' within a cosmology which accommodated witchcraft beliefs. That cosmology was largely defined by the Bible. There are, indeed, interesting parallels between *Macbeth* and the story of Saul and the Witch of Endor in the Book of Samuel (I Samuel XXVIII), a text which was dealt with by nearly every Renaissance treatise on witchcraft. Jane Jack has explored this parallel in an important article, where she writes:

> Like Saul, Macbeth hears from the witches the confirmation of what he most fears. The crisis of the story is the victory of the witches: the resolution of the story is the judgement passed on Macbeth at the end – the same judgement that is passed on Saul: 'So Saul dyed for his transgression, that he committed against the word of the Lord, which he kept not, and in that he sought and asked consel of a familiar spirit' (glossed in Geneva version as a 'witche and sorceress').[17]

Jack goes on to assert the essentially religious tenor of *Macbeth*, a view which most critics of the play seem to hold. Murray, for example, maintains:

> [*Macbeth*] is, if ever a poem were so, a *traditional Catholic Christian poem*, the vitality of which is rooted in an uncompromising medieval faith, and in a prescientific view of the nature of reality. Consequently it preserves in a tremendously powerful and well unified set of images one of the greatest forces in Western European culture, a force which, however alien it may seem to many of us today, we can afford neither to forget, nor to neglect, for it contains, and can still convey, much of the wisdom of human experience.[18]

The 'Christian' interpretation is, I believe, right in so far as it recognises that *Macbeth* can only be understood in relation to a particular cosmology. But Murray, like Jack, attempts to separate religion from politics in a way which was totally foreign to sixteenth- and seventeenth-century thinking. For instance, the Fifth Commandment ('Honour thy father and thy mother' – but Sir Robert Filmer lopped off . . . 'and thy mother'[19]) received new emphasis during this period so as to give religious underpinnings to the patriarchal state.

Indeed, analogical thinking could be used not only to draw close parallels between the law of Moses and the law of the State but also to collapse traditional distinctions. Thus, in *The Six Bookes of the Commonweale* (1586), Bodin rejected Aristotle's distinction between political and domestic hierarchy, claiming that the family 'is the true seminarie and beginning of every Commonweale'.[20] Nor is it surprising that Bodin also wrote an influential attack upon witchcraft, *Démonomanie des Sorciers* (1580). If state and family were founded together, witchcraft founded the antistate together with the antifamily. James I also made the connection between state and family ('By the Law of Nature the King becomes a naturall Father to all his Lieges at his Coronation'[21]) and he too saw witchcraft as the antithesis of both. If the family was theorised as the site of conflict between hierarchy and witchcraft, that was, no doubt, because of its symbolic importance in early modern Europe when, as Natalie Davis writes,

> the nature of political rule and the newer problem of sovereignty were very much at issue. In the little world of the family, with its conspicuous tension between intimacy and power, the larger matters of political and social order could find ready symbolization.[22]

Witchcraft, sovereignty, the family – those concepts map out the ideological terrain of *Macbeth*, a terrain which should be understood as a field of conflict, not a 'given'.

I would argue, then, that Murray is wrong in attempting to collapse the present moment of analysis back into the 'eternity' of a past 'wisdom'. What, after all, are those 'well unified set of images', which give us 'the wisdom of human experience', *about*? 'Unreasoning womanhood', 'eternal motherhood', mind as 'a male quality only', Murray tells us.[23] He points, I believe, to important elements in the play, but he then requires that we *empathise* with its symbolic orderings without reference to those orderings as embodying particular manoeuvres of power. ...

But the play is not, of course, *about* witchcraft, nor does the threat of the Biblical 'Thou shalt not suffer a witch to live' (Exodus, XXII.18) hang over *Macbeth* as it hangs over *The Witch of Edmonton* (1621), for instance. And it cannot be said that the witches in *Macbeth* provide the only explanatory element in the play. If their prophecies provide one motive for the killing of a king, the radical instability of the concept of 'manliness' is sufficient to precipitate the deed. But it would be misleading to interpret this overdetermination as a *conflict* between supernatural and natural modes of explanation, since, within the cultural context, there was no necessity to choose between those modes. (For example, Mother Sawyer in *The Witch of Edmonton* is at first abused as a witch merely because, as she complains, 'I am poor, deform'd and ignorant' (II.i.3); but the fact that she is presented sympathetically as a scapegoat – the natural explanation – is not seen as contradicting the fact that she becomes a witch – the supernatural explanation – and therefore presumably 'deserves' her death.) Nevertheless the coexistence of those modes suggests that the structural closures which I have been examining do not preclude a problematic relation between 'highly' and 'holily' (I.v.17–18).

From *Focus on 'Macbeth'*, ed. John Russell Brown (London, 1982), pp. 189–92, 193–200, 201–4, 206.

NOTES

[This essay draws upon history and anthropology to construct a framework within which the roles of the witches may be understood in relation to those of the women characters in the play. A feminist and cultural-materialist politics leads Peter Stallybrass to reject the suggestion that *Macbeth* presents 'the wisdom of human experience'. In this slightly shortened reprint the notes have been abbreviated to necessary references; *Macbeth* is quoted from *William Shakespeare: The Complete Works*, ed. Peter Alexander (London, 1951). Ed.]

1. T. A. Spalding, *Elizabethan Demonology* (1880); W. C. Curry, *Shakespeare's Philosophical Patterns* (Louisiana, 1937).

2. Bronislaw Malinowski, quoted by Philip Mayer, 'Witches', in Max Marwick (ed.), *Witchcraft and Sorcery* (Harmondsworth, 1970), p. 48.

3. Mary Douglas, *Witchcraft Confessions and Accusations* (London, 1970), p. xxx.

4. Mary Douglas, *Purity and Danger: an analysis of concepts of pollution and taboo* (London, 1978), p. 35.

5. G. L. Kittredge, *Witchcraft in Old and New England* (Cambridge, Mass., 1929), pp. 226, 229, 260–1.

6. 'An Act against seditious words and rumours uttered against the Queen's most excellent Majesty' (23 Eliz., c.2), quoted in Barbara Rosen (ed.), *Witchcraft* (London, 1969), p. 56.

7. *Newes from Scotland* (n.d.), sig. B2.

8. Christina Larner, 'James VI and I and Witchcraft', in *The Reign of James VI and I*, ed. Alan G. R. Smith (London, 1973).

9. Stuart Clark, in Sidney Anglo (ed.), *The Damned Art* (London, 1977), pp. 156–7, 175–7.

10. Raphael Holinshed, *Chronicles of Scotland*, quoted in Kenneth Muir (ed.), *Macbeth*, New Arden edn (London, 1972), p. 167. All Holinshed quotations are from this edition.

11. *Basilikon Doron*, in *The Political Works of James I*, ed. Charles H. McIlwain (Cambridge, Mass., 1918), pp. 18–19.

12. Henry Paul, *The Royal Play of Macbeth* (New York, 1950), p. 163.

13. Reginald Scot, *The Discoverie of Witchcraft*, ed. Montague Summers (London, 1930), p. 1.

14. Mark Rose, *Shakespearean Design* (Cambridge, Mass., 1972), p. 88.

15. Heinrich Krämer and Jacob Sprenger, *Malleus Maleficarum*, in *Witchcraft in Europe 1100–1700: a documentary history*, ed. A. C. Kors and E. Peters (Philadelphia, 1972), p. 121.

16. Curry, *Shakespeare's Philosophical Patterns*, p. 89.

17. Jane H. Jack, '*Macbeth*, King James and the Bible', *English Literary History*, 22 (1955), 182–3.

18. W. A. Murray, 'Why was Duncan's Blood Golden?', *Shakespeare Survey*, 19 (1966), 43.

19. Sir Robert Filmer, *Patriarcha and Other Political Works*, ed. Peter Laslett (Oxford, 1969), pp. 188, 269, 289.

20. Jean Bodin, *The Six Bookes of a Commonweale*, trans. Richard Knolles (1606), ed. Kenneth D. McRae (Cambridge, Mass., 1962), I.ii, p. 8.

21. *Political Works of James I*, p. 55.

22. Natalie Z. Davis, 'Women on Top: symbolic sexual inversion and political disorder in Early Modern Europe', in *The Reversible World: Symbolic Inversion in Art and Society*, ed. Barbara B. Babcock (Ithaca, 1978), p. 150.

23. Murray, 'Why was Duncan's Blood Golden?', p. 39.

3

The Character of Lady Macbeth

SIGMUND FREUD

... We may take as an example of a person who collapses on reaching success, after striving for it with single-minded energy, the figure of Shakespeare's Lady Macbeth. Beforehand there is no hesitation, no sign of any internal conflict in her, no endeavour but that of overcoming the scruples of her ambitious and yet tender-minded husband. She is ready to sacrifice even her womanliness to her murderous intention, without reflecting on the decisive part which this womanliness must play when the question afterwards arises of preserving the aim of her ambition, which has been attained through a crime.

> Come, you spirits
> That tend on mortal thoughts, unsex me here
> ... Come to my woman's breasts,
> And take my milk for gall, you murdering ministers!
>
> (I.v.)
>
> ... I have given suck, and know
> How tender 'tis to love the babe that milks me:
> I would, while it was smiling in my face,
> Have pluck'd my nipple from his boneless gums,
> And dashed the brains out, had I so sworn as you
> Have done to this.
>
> (I.vii.)

One solitary faint stirring of reluctance comes over her before the deed:

> ... Had he not resembled
> My father as he slept, I had done it ...
>
> (II.ii)

Then, when she has become Queen through the murder of Duncan, she betrays for a moment something like disappointment, something like disillusionment. We cannot tell why.

> ... Nought's had, all's spent,
> Where our desire is got without content:
> 'Tis safer to be that which we destroy,
> Than by destruction dwell in doubtful joy.
>
> (III.ii)

Nevertheless, she holds out. In the banqueting scene which follows on these words, she alone keeps her head, cloaks her husband's state of confusion and finds a pretext for dismissing the guests. And then she disappears from view. We next see her in the sleep-walking scene in the last Act, fixated to the impressions of the night of the murder. Once again, as then, she seeks to put heart into her husband: 'Fie, my lord, fie! a soldier, and afeard? What need we fear who knows it, when none can call our power to account?' (V.i).

She hears the knocking at the door, which terrified her husband after the deed. But at the same time she strives to 'undo the deed which cannot be undone'. She washes her hands, which are blood-stained and smell of blood, and is conscious of the futility of the attempt. She who had seemed so remorseless seems to have been borne down by remorse. When she dies, Macbeth, who meanwhile has become as inexorable as she had been in the beginning, can only find a brief epitaph for her:

> She should have died hereafter;
> There would have been a time for such a word.
>
> (V.v)

And now we ask ourselves what it was that broke this character which had seemed forged from the toughest metal? Is it only disillusionment – the different aspect shown by the accomplished deed – and are we to infer that even in Lady Macbeth an originally gentle and womanly nature had been worked up to a concentration and high tension which could not endure for long, or ought we to seek for signs of a deeper motivation which will make this collapse more humanly intelligible to us?

It seems to me impossible to come to any decision. Shakespeare's *Macbeth* is a *pièce d'occasion*, written for the accession of James, who had hitherto been King of Scotland. The plot was ready-made, and had been handled by other contemporary writers, whose work Shakespeare probably made use of in his customary manner. It offered remarkable analogies to the actual situation. The 'virginal' Elizabeth, of whom it was rumoured that she had never been capable of child-bearing and who had once described herself as 'a barren stock',[1] in an anguished outcry at the news of James's birth, was obliged by this very childlessness of hers to make the Scottish king her successor. And he was the son of the Mary Stuart whose execution she, even though reluctantly, had ordered, and who, in spite of the clouding of their relations by political concerns, was nevertheless of her blood and might be called her guest.

The accession of James I was like a demonstration of the curse of unfruitfulness and the blessings of continuous generation. And the action of Shakespeare's *Macbeth* is based on this same contrast.

The Weird Sisters assured Macbeth that he himself should be king, but to Banquo they promised that his children should succeed to the crown. Macbeth is incensed by this decree of destiny. He is not content with the satisfaction of his own ambition. He wants to found a dynasty – not to have murdered for the benefit of strangers. This point is overlooked if Shakespeare's play is regarded only as a tragedy of ambition. It is clear that Macbeth cannot live for ever, and thus there is but one way for him to invalidate the part of the prophecy which opposes him – namely, to have children himself who can succeed him. And he seems to expect them from his indomitable wife:

> Bring forth men-children only!
> For thy undaunted mettle should compose
> Nothing but males. . . .
>
> (I.vii)

And equally it is clear that if he is deceived in this expectation he must submit to destiny; otherwise his actions lose all purpose and are transformed into the blind fury of one doomed to destruction, who is resolved to destroy beforehand all that he can reach. We watch Macbeth pass through this development, and at the height of the tragedy we hear Macduff's shattering cry, which has so often been recognised to be ambiguous and which may perhaps contain the key to the change in Macbeth:

> He has no children!
> (IV.iii)

There is no doubt that this means: 'Only because he is himself childless could he murder my children.' But more may be implied in it, and above all it might lay bare the deepest motive which not only forces Macbeth to go far beyond his own nature, but also touches the hard character of his wife at its only weak point. If one surveys the whole play from the summit marked by these words of Macduff's, one sees that it is sown with references to the father-children relation. The murder of the kindly Duncan is little else than parricide; in Banquo's case, Macbeth kills the father while the son escapes him; and in Macduff's, he kills the children because the father has fled from him. A bloody child, and then a crowned one, are shown him by the witches in the apparition scene; the armed head which is seen earlier is no doubt Macbeth himself. But in the background rises the sinister form of the avenger, Macduff, who is himself an exception to the laws of generation, since he was not born of his mother but ripp'd from her womb.

It would be a perfect example of poetic justice in the manner of the talion if the childlessness of Macbeth and the barrenness of his Lady were the punishment for their crimes against the sanctity of genera-tion – if Macbeth could not become a father because he had robbed children of their father and a father of his children, and if Lady Macbeth suffered the unsexing she had demanded of the spirits of murder. I believe Lady Macbeth's illness, the transformation of her callousness into penitence, could be explained directly as a reaction to her childlessness, by which she is convinced of her impotence against the decrees of nature, and at the same time reminded that it is through her own fault if her crime has been robbed of the better part of its fruits.

In Holinshed's *Chronicle* (1577), from which Shakespeare took the plot of *Macbeth*, Lady Macbeth is only once mentioned as the ambitious wife who instigates her husband to murder in order that she may herself become queen. There is no mention of her subse-quent fate and of the development of her character. On the other hand, it would seem that the change of Macbeth's character into a bloodthirsty tyrant is ascribed to the same motives as we have suggested here. For in Holinshed *ten years* pass between the murder of Duncan, through which Macbeth becomes king, and his further misdeeds; and in these ten years he is shown as a stern but just ruler. It is not until after this lapse of time that the change begins in him, under the influence of the tormenting fear that the prophecy to Banquo may be fulfilled just as the prophecy of his own destiny has been. Only then does he contrive the murder of Banquo, and, as in Shakespeare, is driven from one crime to another. It is not expressly stated in Holinshed that it was his childlessness which urged him to these courses, but enough time and room is given for that plausible motive. Not so in Shakespeare. Events crowd upon us in the tragedy with breathless haste so that, to judge by the statements made by the characters in it, the course of its action covers about *one week*. This acceleration takes the ground from under all our constructions of the motives for the change in the characters of Macbeth and his wife. There is no time for a long-drawn-out disappointment of their hopes of offspring to break the woman down and drive the man to defiant rage; and the contradiction remains that though so many subtle inter-relations in the plot, and between it and its occasion, point to a common origin of them in the theme of childlessness, nevertheless the economy of time in the tragedy expressly precludes a development of character from any motives but those inherent in the action itself.

What, however, these motives can have been which in so short a space of time could turn the hesitating, ambitious man into an unbridled tyrant, and his steely-hearted instigator into a sick woman gnawed by remorse, it is, in my view, impossible to guess. We must, I think, give up any hope of penetrating the triple layer of obscurity into which the bad preservation of the text, the unknown intention of the dramatist, and the hidden purport of the legend have become condensed. But I should not subscribe to the objection that investigations like these are idle in face of the powerful effect which the tragedy has upon the spectator. The dramatist can indeed, during the representation, overwhelm us by his art and paralyse our powers of reflection; but he cannot prevent us from attempting subsequently to grasp its effect by studying its psychological mechanism. Nor does the contention that a dramatist is at liberty to shorten at will the natural chronology of the events he brings before us, if by the sacrifice of common probability he can enhance the dramatic effect, seem to me relevant in this instance. For such a sacrifice is justified only when it merely interferes with probability, and not when it breaks the causal connection; moreover, the dramatic effect would hardly have suffered if the passage of time had been left indeterminate, instead of being expressly limited to a few days.

One is so unwilling to dismiss a problem like that of *Macbeth* as insoluble that I will venture to bring up a fresh point, which may offer another way out of the difficulty. Ludwig Jekels, in a recent Shakespearean study,[2] thinks he has discovered a particular technique of the poet's, and this might apply to *Macbeth*. He believes that Shakespeare often splits a character up into two personages, which, taken separately, are not completely understandable and do not become so until they are brought together once more into a unity. This might be so with Macbeth and Lady Macbeth. In that case it would of course be pointless to regard her as an independent character and seek to discover the motives for her change, without considering the Macbeth who completes her. I shall not follow this clue any further, but I should, nevertheless, like to point out something which strikingly confirms this view: the germs of fear which break out in Macbeth on the night of the murder do not develop further in *him* but in *her*. It is he who has the hallucination of the dagger before the crime; but it is she who afterwards falls ill of a mental disorder. It is he who after the murder hears the cry in the house: 'Sleep no more! Macbeth does murder sleep...' and so 'Macbeth shall sleep no more'; but we never hear that *he* slept no more, while the Queen, as we see, rises from her bed and, talking in her sleep, betrays her guilt. It is he who stands helpless with bloody hands, lamenting that 'all great Neptune's ocean' will not wash them clean, while she comforts him: 'A little water clears us of this deed'; but later it is she who washes her hands for a quarter of an hour and cannot get rid of the bloodstains: 'All the perfumes of Arabia will not sweeten this little hand.' Thus what he feared in his pangs of conscience is fulfilled in her; she becomes all remorse and he all defiance. Together they exhaust the possibilities of reaction to the crime, like two disunited parts of a single psychical individuality, and it may be that they are both copied from a single prototype.

From Sigmund Freud, 'Some Character-Types Met with in Psychoanalytic Work', in *The Standard Edition of the Complete Psychological Works*, ed. James Strachey, vol. 14 (London, 1957), pp. 318–24.

NOTES

[These remarks by Freud are from one of three brief studies published in 1916 and translated as 'Some Character-Types Met with in Psychoanalytic Work'. At this time Freud had been working out ideas on repression, narcissism, the unconscious and mourning and melancholia. The thought that Lady Macbeth is incoherent as a character runs counter to most traditional criticism, challenging readers to regard the play as an organisation of ideas about gender rather than insights into individuals. The note in brackets below is by Freud's English editors. Freud does not say from which edition he is quoting *Macbeth*. Ed.]

1. Cf. *Macbeth*, III.i:

   Upon my head they placed a fruitless crown,
   And put a barren sceptre in my gripe,
   Thence to be wrenched with an unlineal hand,
   No son of mine succeeding...

2. [This does not appear to have been published. In a later paper on *Macbeth* Jekels (1917) barely refers to this theory, apart from quoting the present paragraph. In a still later paper, on 'The Psychology of Comedy', Jekels (1926) returns to the subject, but again very briefly.]

4

'The witches are the heroines of the piece ...'

TERRY EAGLETON

Even those who know very little about Shakespeare might be vaguely aware that his plays value social order and stability, and that they are written with an extraordinary eloquence, one metaphor breeding another in an apparently unstaunchable flow of what modern theorists might call 'textual productivity'. The problem is that these two aspects of Shakespeare are in potential conflict with one another. For a stability of signs – each word securely in place, each signifier (mark or sound) corresponding to its signified (or meaning) – is an integral part of any social order: settled meanings, shared definitions and regularities of grammar both reflect, and help to constitute, a well-ordered political state. Yet it is all this which Shakespeare's flamboyant punning, troping and riddling threaten to put into question. His belief in social stability is jeopardised by the very language in which it is articulated. It would seem, then, that the very act of writing implies for Shakespeare an epistemology (or theory of knowledge) at odds with his political ideology. This is a deeply embarrassing dilemma, and it is not surprising that much of Shakespeare's drama is devoted to figuring out strategies for resolving it.

To any unprejudiced reader – which would seem to exclude Shakespeare himself, his contemporary audiences and almost all literary critics – it is surely clear that positive value in *Macbeth* lies with the three witches. The witches are the heroines of the piece, however little the play itself recognises the fact, and however much the critics may have set out to defame them. It is they who, by releasing ambitious thoughts in Macbeth, expose a reverence for hierarchical social order for what it is, as the pious self-deception of a society based on routine oppression and incessant warfare. The witches are exiles from that violent order, inhabiting their own sisterly community on its shadowy borderlands, refusing all truck with its tribal bickerings and military honours. It is their riddling, ambiguous speech (they 'palter with us in a double sense') which promises to subvert this structure: their teasing word-play infiltrates and undermines Macbeth from within, revealing in him a lack which hollows his being into desire. The witches signify a realm of non-meaning and poetic play which hovers at the work's margins, one which has its own kind of truth; and their words to Macbeth catalyse this region of otherness and desire within himself, so that by the end of the play it has flooded up from within him to shatter and engulf his previously assured identity. In this sense the witches figure as the 'unconscious' of the drama, that which must be exiled and repressed as dangerous but which is always likely to return with a vengeance. That unconscious is a discourse in which meaning falters and slides, in which firm definitions are dissolved and binary oppositions eroded: fair is foul and foul is fair, nothing is but what is not. Androgynous (bearded women), multiple (three-in-one) and 'imperfect speakers', the witches strike at the stable social, sexual and linguistic forms which the society of the play needs in order to survive. They perform a 'deed without a name', and Macbeth's own actions, once influenced by them, become such that 'Tongue nor heart / Cannot conceive nor name'. The physical fluidity of the three sisters becomes inscribed in Macbeth's own restless desire, continually pursuing the pure being of kingship but at each step ironically unravelling that very possibility: 'To be thus is nothing, / But to be safely thus.' Macbeth ends up chasing an identity which continually eludes him; he becomes a floating signifier in ceaseless, doomed pursuit of an anchoring signified:

> Life's but a walking shadow, a poor player,
> That struts and frets his hour upon the stage,
> And then is heard no more; it is a tale
> Told by an idiot, full of sound and fury,
> Signifying nothing.
>
> (V.v.24–8)

He is reduced to a ham actor, unable to identify with his role.

As the most fertile force in the play, the witches inhabit an anarchic, richly ambiguous zone both in and out of official society: they live in their own world but intersect with Macbeth's. They are poets, prophetesses and devotees of female cult, radical separatists who scorn male power and lay bare the hollow sound and fury at its heart. Their words and bodies mock rigorous boundaries and make sport of fixed positions, unhinging received meanings as they dance, dissolve and re-materialise. But official society can only ever imagine its radical 'other' as chaos rather than creativity, and is thus bound to define the sisters as evil. Foulness – a political order which thrives on bloodshed – believes itself fair, whereas the witches do not so much invert this opposition as deconstruct it. Macbeth himself fears the troubling of exact definitions: to be authentically human is, in his view, to be creatively constrained, fixed and framed by certain precise bonds of hierarchical allegiance. Beyond these lies the dissolute darkness of the witches into which, by murdering Duncan, he will catapult himself at a stroke. To transgress these determining bonds, for Macbeth, is to become less than human in trying to become more, a mere self-cancelling liberty:

> I dare do all that may become a man;
> Who dares do more is none.
>> (I.vii.46–7)

Too much inverts itself into nothing at all. Later Ross will speak of 'float[ing] upon a wild and violent sea, / Each way and none', meaning that to move in all directions at once is to stand still.

Lady Macbeth holds the opposite view: transgression, the ceaseless surpassing of limits, is for her the very mark of the human:

> When you durst do it, then you were a man;
> And to be more than what you were, you would
> Be so much more the man.
>> (I.vii.49–51)

She herself crosses the strict divide of gender roles and cries out to be unsexed, flouting Angelo's paternalistic advice to Isabella in *Measure for Measure*:

> Be that you are,
> That is, a woman; if you be more, you're none ...
>> (II.iv.134–5)

Like most of Shakespeare's villains, in short, Lady Macbeth is a bourgeois individualist, for whom traditional ties of rank and kinship are less constitutive of personal identity than mere obstacles to be surmounted in the pursuit of one's private ends. But the witches are hardly to be blamed for this, whatever Macbeth's own jaundiced view of the matter. For one thing they live in community, not as individual entrepreneurs of the self; and unlike the Macbeths they are indifferent to political power because they have no truck with linear time, which is always, so to speak, on the side of Caesar.

The Macbeths' impulse to transgress inhabits history: it is an endless expansion of the self in a single trajectory, an unslakable thirst for some ultimate mastery which will never come. The witches' subversiveness moves within cyclical time, centred on dance, the moon, pre-vision and verbal repetition, inimical to linear history and its imperial themes of sexual reproduction. It is such lineage – the question of which particular male will inherit political power – which they garble and confound in their address to Macbeth and Banquo, as well as in their most lethal piece of double-talk of all: 'none of woman born shall harm Macbeth'. Like the unconscious, the witches know no narrative; but once the creative dissolution they signify is inflected *within* the political system, it can always take the form of a 'freedom' which remains enslaved to the imperatives of power, a desire which merely reproduces, sexually and politically, the same old story and the same oppressive law. There is a style of transgression which is play and poetic non-sense, a dark carnival in which all formal values are satirised and deranged, and there is the different but related disruptiveness of bourgeois individualist appetite, which, in its ruthless drive to be all, sunders every constraint and lapses back into nothing. Such ambition is as self-undoing as the porter's drink, provoking desire but taking away the performance: unlike the fruitful darkness of the witches, it is a nothing from which nothing can come.

This ambivalence of transgression is well captured in the *Communist Manifesto*. The bourgeoisie, Marx and Engels write, cannot exist without constantly revolutionising all social relations:

> Constant revolutionizing of production, uninterrupted disturbance of all social conditions, everlasting uncertainty and agitation distinguish the bourgeois epoch from all earlier ones. All fixed, fast-frozen relations, with their train of ancient and venerable prejudices and opinions, are swept away, all new-formed ones become antiquated before they can ossify. All that is solid melts into air, all that is holy is

profaned, and man is at last compelled to face with sober senses his real conditions of life, and his relations with his kind.[1]

'All that is solid melts into air, all that is holy is profaned': this is the positive trespassing and travestying of the witches, who dissolve into thin air and disfigure all sacred values. Yet this liquidation of all 'fixed, fast-frozen relations' is, in the case of the bourgeoisie, finally self-destructive, breeding new forms of exploitation which in the end will undo it. Like Macbeth, the bourgeoisie will become entangled in its own excess, giving birth to its own gravedigger (the working class), dissolving away that obstacle to historical development which is itself, and dying of its own too much. The universal wolf of appetite, as Ulysses remarks in *Troilus and Cressida*, 'Must make perforce an universal prey, / And last eat up himself' (I.iii.123–4). Lady Macbeth is akin to the three sisters in celebrating female power, but in modern parlance she is a 'bourgeois' feminist who strives to outdo in domination and virility the very male system which subordinates her. Even so, it is hard to see why her bloodthirsty talk of dashing out babies' brains is any more 'unnatural' than skewering an enemy soldier's guts. Meek women, military carnage and aristocratic titles are supposed by the play to be natural; witches and regicide are not. Yet this opposition will not hold even within *Macbeth*'s own terms, since the 'unnatural' – Macbeth's lust for power – is disclosed by the witches as already lurking within the 'natural' – the routine state of cut-throat rivalry between noblemen. Nature harbours the unnatural within its bosom, and does so as one of its conditions of being: since Nature can be defined only by reference to its so-called perversions, Macbeth is right to believe that nothing is but what is not. Nature, to be normative, must already include the possibility of its own perversion, just as a sign can be roughly defined as anything which can be used for the purpose of lying. A mark which did not structurally contain the capacity to be abused would not be called a sign. The fact that Macbeth's conqueror was born by caesarean section (that is, 'unnaturally') is an 'unnatural', patriarchal repression of men's dependency on women; but the witches do well to steer clear of sexual reproduction in a society where birth determines whom you may 'naturally' exploit, dispossess or defer to.

In killing Duncan, symbol of the body politic, Macbeth is, in the play's ideological terms, striking at the physical root of his own life, so that the act of regicide is also a form of bodily self-estrangement.

In a graphic gesture of self-division, his hand will try to clutch a dagger bred by his own brain. Language – the equivocal enigmas of the witches – overwhelms and dismembers the body; desire inflates consciousness to the point where it dissevers itself from sensuous constraints and comes to consume itself in a void. When language is cut loose from reality, signifiers split from signifieds, the result is a radical fissure between consciousness and material life. Macbeth will end up as a bundle of broken signifiers, his body reduced to a blind automaton of battle; his sleepwalking wife disintegrates into fragments of hallucinated speech and mindless physical action. Duncan's commendation of the bleeding sergeant ('So well thy words become thee as thy wounds') suggests, by contrast, an organic unity of body and speech. The body is a duplicitous signifier, sometimes transparently expressive of an inner essence, sometimes, as with Macbeth's countenance, a cryptic text to be deciphered. As we shall see throughout this study, Shakespeare feels the need to integrate a potentially overweening consciousness within the body's sure limits, a process which is for him inseparable from the integration of individuals into the body politic. It also involves a restabilising of the sign, restoring floating signifiers to their appropriate signifieds, for meaning is the 'spirit' of words which should find true incarnation in their material forms. The problem is how to do all this without suppressing what is productive about individual energies, and suggestive about the sliding, metaphorical word.

The Macbeths are finally torn apart in the contradiction between body and language, between the frozen bonds of traditional allegiance and the unassuageable dynamic of desire. The witches experience no such conflict because their very bodies are not static but mutable, melting as breath into the wind, ambivalently material and immaterial, and so, as 'breath' suggests, with all the protean quality of language itself. One exit-route from the tragedy of the play, in short, would be to have a different sort of body altogether, one which had escaped from singular identity into diffusion and plurality. Shakespeare will return to this idea in his very last drama in the figure of Ariel. But *Macbeth* fears this feminine fluidity as political anarchy, viewing diffusion as disruption. One of its more creditable reasons for doing so is that it is worried by the closeness of this fruitful interchangeability of signs, roles and bodies to a certain destructive tendency in bourgeois thought which levels all differences to the same dead level, in the anarchy and arbitrariness of the market-place.

From Terry Eagleton, *William Shakespeare* (Oxford, 1986), pp. 1–8.

NOTES

[Terry Eagleton admits that the play may not recognise that the witches are its real heroines. But then, is it necessary to read the play in its own terms? May not a reading *against the grain* enable us to understand better? Eagleton's argument that the riddling, ambiguous speech of the witches may undermine the stability claimed by an oppressive state draws upon a characteristic perception of poststructuralism, one pursued in other extracts below. Shakespeare's plays are quoted from *The Complete Works*, ed. Peter Alexander (London and Glasgow, 1951). Ed.]

1. Karl Marx and Friedrich Engels, *Selected Works* (London, 1968), p. 38.

5

'Born of woman': Fantasies of Maternal Power in 'Macbeth'

JANET ADELMAN

... In the figures of Macbeth, Lady Macbeth, and the witches, the play gives us images of a masculinity and a femininity that are terribly disturbed; this disturbance seems to me both the cause and the consequence of the murder of Duncan. In *Hamlet*, Shakespeare had reconstructed the Fall as the death of the ideal father; here, he constructs a revised version in which the Fall is the death of the ideally androgynous parent. For Duncan combines in himself the attributes of both father and mother: he is the centre of authority, the source of lineage and honour, the giver of name and gift; but he is also the source of all nurturance, planting the children to his throne and making them grow. He is the father as androgynous parent from whom, singly, all good can be imagined to flow, the source of a benign and empowering nurturance the opposite of that imaged in the witches' poisonous cauldron and Lady Macbeth's gall-filled breasts. Such a father does away with any need for a mother: he is the image of both parents in one, threatening aspects of each controlled by the presence of the other. When he is gone, 'The wine of life is drawn, and the mere lees / Is left this vault to brag of' (II.iii.93–4): nurturance itself is spoiled, as all the play's imagery of poisoned chalices and interrupted feasts implies. In his absence male and female break apart, the female becoming merely helpless or merely poisonous and the male merely bloodthirsty; the harmonious relation of the genders imaged in Duncan fails.

In *Hamlet*, the absence of the ideal protecting father brings the son face to face with maternal power. The absence of Duncan similarly unleashes the power of the play's malevolent mothers. But this father-king seems strikingly absent even before his murder. Heavily idealised, he is nonetheless largely ineffectual: even while he is alive, he is unable to hold his kingdom together, reliant on a series of bloody men to suppress an increasingly successful series of rebellions. The witches are already abroad in his realm; they in fact constitute our introduction to that realm. Duncan, not Macbeth, is the first person to echo them ('When the battle's lost and won' [I.i.4]; 'What he hath lost, noble Macbeth hath won' [I.ii.69]). The witches' sexual ambiguity terrifies: Banquo says of them, 'You should be women, / And yet your beards forbid me to interpret / That you are so' (I.iii.45–7). Is their androgyny the shadow-side of the King's, enabled perhaps by his failure to maintain a protective masculine authority? Is their strength a consequence of his weakness? (This is the configuration of *Cymbeline*, where the power of the witch-queen-stepmother is so dependent on the failure of Cymbeline's masculine authority that she obligingly dies when that authority returns to him.) Banquo's question to the witches may ask us to hear a counterquestion about Duncan, who should be man. For Duncan's androgyny is the object of enormous ambivalence: idealised for his nurturing paternity, he is nonetheless killed for his womanish softness, his childish trust, his inability to read men's minds in their faces, his reliance on the fighting of sons who can rebel against him. Macbeth's description of the dead Duncan – 'his silver skin lac'd with his golden blood' (II.iii.110) – makes him into a virtual icon of kingly worth; but other images surrounding his death make him into an emblem not of masculine authority, but of female vulnerability. As he moves toward the murder, Macbeth first imagines himself the allegorical figure of murder, as though to absolve himself of the responsibility of choice. But the figure of murder then fuses with that of Tarquin:

> wither'd Murther,
> . . . thus with his stealthy pace,
> With Tarquin's ravishing strides, towards his design
> Moves like a ghost.
>
> (II.i.52–6)

These lines figure the murder as a display of male sexual aggression against a passive female victim: murder here becomes rape; Macbeth's victim becomes not the powerful male figure of the king, but the helpless Lucrece. Hardened by Lady Macbeth to regard maleness and violence as equivalent, that is, Macbeth responds to Duncan's idealised milky gentleness as though it were evidence of his femaleness. The horror of this gender transformation, as well as the horror of the murder, is implicit in Macduff's identification of the king's body as a new Gorgon ('Approach the chamber, and destroy your sight / With a new Gorgon' [II.iii.70–1]). The power of this image lies partly in its suggestion that Duncan's bloodied body, with its multiple wounds, has been revealed as female and hence blinding to his sons: as if the threat all along was that Duncan would be revealed as female and that this revelation would rob his sons of his masculine protection and hence of their own masculinity.

In *King Lear*, the abdication of protective paternal power seems to release the destructive power of a female chaos imaged not only in Goneril and Regan, but also in the storm on the heath. Macbeth virtually alludes to Lear's storm as he approaches the witches in Act IV, conjuring them to answer though they 'untie the winds, and let them fight / Against the Churches', though the 'waves / Confound and swallow navigation up', though 'the treasure / Of Nature's germens tumble all together / Even till destruction sicken' (IV.i.52–60; see *King Lear*, III.ii.1–9). The witches merely implicit on Lear's heath have become in *Macbeth* embodied agents of storm and disorder, and they are there from the start. Their presence suggests that the absence of the father that unleashes female chaos (as in *Lear*) has already happened at the beginning of *Macbeth*; that absence is merely made literal in Macbeth's murder of Duncan at the instigation of female forces. For this father-king cannot protect his sons from powerful mothers, and it is the son's – and the play's – revenge to kill him, or, more precisely, to kill him first and love him after, paying him back for his excessively 'womanish' trust and then memorialising him as the ideal androgynous parent. The reconstitution of manhood becomes a central problem of the play in part, I think, because the vision of manhood embodied in Duncan has already failed at the play's beginning.

The witches constitute our introduction to the realm of maternal malevolence unleashed by the loss of paternal protection; as soon as Macbeth meets them, he becomes (in Hecate's probably non-Shakespearean words) their 'wayward son' (III.v.11). This maternal malevolence is given its most horrifying expression in Shakespeare in the image through which Lady Macbeth secures her control over Macbeth:

> I have given suck, and know
> How tender 'tis to love the babe that milks me:
> I would, while it was smiling in my face,
> Have pluck'd my nipple from his boneless gums,
> And dash'd the brains out, had I so sworn
> As you have done to this.
>
> (I.vii.54–9)

The image of murderously disrupted nurturance is the psychic equivalence of the witches' poisonous cauldron; both function to subject Macbeth's will to female forces. For the play strikingly constructs the fantasy of subjection to maternal malevolence in two parts, in the witches and in Lady Macbeth, and then persistently identifies the two parts as one. Through this identification, Shakespeare in effect locates the source of his culture's fear of witchcraft in individual human history, in the infant's long dependence on female figures felt as all-powerful: what the witches suggest about the vulnerability of men to female power on the cosmic plane, Lady Macbeth doubles on the psychological plane.

Lady Macbeth's power as a female temptress allies her in a general way with the witches as soon as we see her. The specifics of that implied alliance begin to emerge as she attempts to harden herself in preparation for hardening her husband: the disturbance of gender that Banquo registers when he first meets the witches is played out in psychological terms in Lady Macbeth's attempt to unsex herself. Calling on spirits ambiguously allied with the witches themselves, she phrases this unsexing as the undoing of her own bodily maternal function:

> Come, you Spirits
> That tend on mortal thoughts, unsex me here,
> And fill me, from the crown to the toe, top-full
> Of direst cruelty! make thick my blood,
> Stop up th'access and passage to remorse;
> That no compunctious visitings of Nature
> Shake my fell purpose, nor keep peace between
> Th'effect and it! Come to my woman's breasts,
> And take my milk for gall, you murth'ring ministers.
>
> (I.v.40–8)

In the play's context of unnatural births, the thickening of the blood and the stopping up of access and passage to remorse begin to sound like attempts to undo reproductive functioning and perhaps to stop the menstrual blood that is the sign of its potential. The metaphors in which Lady Macbeth frames the stopping up of remorse, that is, suggest that she imagines an attack on the reproductive passages of her own body, on what makes her specifically female. And as she invites the spirits to her breasts, she reiterates the centrality of the attack specifically on maternal function: needing to undo the 'milk of human kindness' (I.v.18) in Macbeth, she imagines an attack on her own literal milk, its transformation into gall. This imagery locates the horror of the scene in Lady Macbeth's unnatural abrogation of her maternal function. But latent within this image of unsexing is the horror of the maternal function itself. Most modern editors follow Johnson in glossing 'take my milk for gall' as 'take my milk in exchange for gall', imagining in effect that the spirits empty out the natural maternal fluid and replace it with the unnatural and poisonous one.[1] But perhaps Lady Macbeth is asking the spirits to take her milk *as* gall, to nurse from her breast and find in her milk their sustaining poison. Here the milk itself is the gall; no transformation is necessary. In these lines Lady Macbeth focuses the culture's fear of maternal nursery – a fear reflected, for example, in the common worries about the various ills (including female blood itself) that could be transmitted through nursing and in the sometime identification of colostrum as witch's milk. In so far as her milk itself nurtures the evil spirits, Lady Macbeth localises the image of maternal danger, inviting the identification of her maternal function itself with that of the witch. For she here invites precisely that nursing of devil-imps so central to the current understanding of witchcraft that the presence of supernumerary teats alone was often taken as sufficient evidence that one was a witch. Lady Macbeth and the witches fuse at this moment, and they fuse through the image of perverse nursery.

It is characteristic of the play's division of labour between Lady Macbeth and the witches that she, rather than they, is given the imagery of perverse nursery traditionally attributed to the witches. The often noted alliance between Lady Macbeth and the witches constructs malignant female power both in the cosmos and in the family; it in effect adds the whole weight of the spiritual order to the condemnation of Lady Macbeth's insurrection. But despite the superior cosmic status of the witches, Lady Macbeth seems to me finally the more frightening figure. . . . For Shakespeare's witches are both smaller and greater than their Continental sisters: on the one hand, more the representation of English homebodies with relatively small concerns; on the other, more the incarnation of literary or mythic fates or sybils, given the power not only to predict but to enforce the future. But the staples of Continental witchcraft belief are not altogether missing from the play: for the most part, they are transferred away from the witches and recur as the psychological issues evoked by Lady Macbeth in her relation to Macbeth. She becomes the inheritor of the realm of primitive relational and bodily disturbance: of infantile vulnerability to maternal power, of dismemberment and its developmentally later equivalent, castration. Lady Macbeth brings the witches' power home: they get the cosmic apparatus, she gets the psychic force. That Lady Macbeth is the more frightening figure – and was so, I suspect, even before belief in witchcraft had declined – suggests the firmly domestic and psychological basis of Shakespeare's imagination.

The fears of female coercion, female definition of the male, that are initially located cosmically in the witches thus find their ultimate locus in the figure of Lady Macbeth, whose attack on Macbeth's virility is the source of her strength over him and who acquires that strength, I shall argue, partly because she can make him imagine himself as an infant vulnerable to her. In the figure of Lady Macbeth, that is, Shakespeare rephrases the power of the witches as the wife/ mother's power to poison human relatedness at its source; in her, their power of cosmic coercion is rewritten as the power of the mother to misshape or destroy the child. The attack on infants and on the genitals characteristic of Continental witchcraft belief is thus in her returned to its psychological source: in the play these beliefs are localised not in the witches but in the great central scene in which Lady Macbeth persuades Macbeth to the murder of Duncan. In this scene, Lady Macbeth notoriously makes the murder of Duncan the test of Macbeth's virility; if he cannot perform the murder, he is in effect reduced to the helplessness of an infant subject to her rage. She begins by attacking his manhood, making her love for him contingent on the murder that she identifies as equivalent to his male potency: 'From this time / Such I account thy love' (I.vii.38–9); 'When you durst do it, then you were a man' (I.vii.49). In so far as his drunk hope is now 'green and pale' (I.vii.37), he is identified as emasculated, exhibiting the symptoms not only of hangover, but also of the green-sickness, the typical disease of timid young virgin women. Lady Macbeth's argument is, in effect, that any signs of the 'milk of human kindness' (I.v.17) mark him as more womanly than she; she proceeds to enforce his masculinity by demonstrating her willingness to dry up that milk in herself, specifically by destroying her nursing infant in fantasy: 'I would, while it was smiling in my face, / Have pluck'd my nipple from his boneless gums, / And dash'd the brains out' (I.vii.56–8). That this image has no place in the plot, where the Macbeths are strikingly childless, gives some indication of the inner necessity through which it appears. For Lady Macbeth expresses here not only the hardness she imagines to be male, not only her willingness to unmake the most essential maternal relationship; she expresses also a deep fantasy of Macbeth's utter vulnerability to her. As she progresses from questioning Macbeth's masculinity to imagining herself dashing out the brains of her infant son, she articulates a fantasy in which to be less than a man is to become interchangeably a woman or a baby, terribly subject to the wife/ mother's destructive rage.

By evoking this vulnerability, Lady Macbeth acquires a power over Macbeth more absolute than any the witches can achieve. The play's central fantasy of escape from woman seems to me to unfold from this moment; we can see its beginnings in Macbeth's response to Lady Macbeth's evocation of absolute maternal power. Macbeth first responds by questioning the possibility of failure ('If we should fail?' [I.vii.59]). Lady Macbeth counters this fear by inviting Macbeth to share in her fantasy of omnipotent malevolence: 'What cannot you and I perform upon / Th'unguarded Duncan?' (I.vii.70–1). The satiated and sleeping Duncan takes on the vulnerability that Lady Macbeth has just invoked in the image of the feeding, trusting infant; Macbeth releases himself from the image of this vulnerability by sharing in the murder of this innocent. In his elation at this transfer of vulnerability from himself to Duncan, Macbeth imagines Lady Macbeth the mother to infants sharing her hardness, born in effect without vulnerability; in effect, he imagines her as male and then reconstitutes himself as the invulnerable male child of such a mother:

> Bring forth men-children only!
> For thy undaunted mettle should compose
> Nothing but males.
>
> (I.vii.73–5)

Through the double pun on *mettle/metal* and *male/mail*, Lady Macbeth herself becomes virtually male, composed of the hard metal of which the armoured male is made. Her children would necessarily be men, composed of her male mettle, armoured by her mettle, lacking the female inheritance from the mother that would make them vulnerable. The man-child thus brought forth would be no trusting infant; the very phrase *men-children* suggests the presence of the adult man even at birth, hence the undoing of childish vulnerability. The mobility of the imagery – from male infant with his brains dashed out to Macbeth and Lady Macbeth triumphing over the sleeping, trusting Duncan, to the all-male invulnerable man-child, suggests the logic of the fantasy: only the child of an all-male mother is safe. We see here the creation of a defensive fantasy of exemption from the woman's part: as infantile vulnerability is shifted to Duncan, Macbeth creates in himself the image of Lady Macbeth's hardened all-male man-child; in committing the murder, he thus becomes like Richard III, using the bloody axe to free himself in fantasy from the dominion of women, even while apparently carrying out their will.

Macbeth's temporary solution to the infantile vulnerability and maternal malevolence revealed by Lady Macbeth is to imagine Lady Macbeth the all-male mother of invulnerable infants. The final solution, both for Macbeth and for the play itself, though in differing ways, is an even more radical excision of the female: it is to imagine a birth entirely exempt from women, to imagine in effect an all-male family, composed of nothing but males, in which the father is fully restored to power. Overtly, of course, the play denies the possibility of this fantasy: Macduff carries the power of the man not born of woman only through the equivocation of the fiends, their obstetrical joke that quibbles with the meaning of *born* and thus confirms circuitously that all men come from women after all. Even Macbeth, in whom, I think, the fantasy is centrally invested, knows its impossibility: his false security depends exactly on his commonsense assumption that everyone is born of woman. Nonetheless, I shall argue, the play curiously enacts the fantasy that it seems to deny: punishing Macbeth for his participation in a fantasy of escape from the maternal matrix, it nonetheless allows the audience the partial satisfaction of a dramatic equivalent to it. The dual process of repudiation and enactment of the fantasy seems to me to shape the ending of *Macbeth* decisively; I will attempt to trace this process in the rest of this essay.

The witches' prophecy has the immediate force of psychic relevance for Macbeth partly because of the fantasy constructions central to I.vii:

> Be bloody, bold, and resolute: laugh to scorn
> The power of man, for none of woman born
> Shall harm Macbeth.
>
> (IV.i.79–81)

The witches here invite Macbeth to make himself into the bloody and
invulnerable man-child he has created as a defence against maternal
malevolence in I.vii: the man-child ambivalently recalled by the
accompanying apparition of the Bloody Child. For the apparition
alludes at once to the bloody vulnerability of the infant destroyed by
Lady Macbeth and to the bloodthirsty masculinity that seems to
promise escape from this vulnerability, the bloodiness the witches
urge Macbeth to take on. The doubleness of the image epitomises
exactly the doubleness of the prophecy itself: the prophecy constructs Macbeth's invulnerability in effect from the vulnerability of
all other men, a vulnerability dependent on their having been born of
woman. Macbeth does not question this prophecy, even after the
experience of Birnam Wood should have taught him better, partly
because it so perfectly meets his needs: in encouraging him to 'laugh
to scorn / The power of men', the prophecy seems to grant him
exemption from the condition of all men, who bring with them the
liabilities inherent in their birth. As Macbeth carries the prophecy as
a shield onto the battlefield, his confidence in his own invulnerability
increasingly reveals his sense of his own exemption from the universal
human condition. Repeated seven times, the phrase *born to woman*
with its variants begins to carry for Macbeth the meaning 'vulnerable',
as though vulnerability itself is the taint deriving from woman; his own
invulnerability comes therefore to stand as evidence for his exemption from that taint. This is the subterranean logic of Macbeth's
words to Young Siward immediately after Macbeth has killed him:

> Thou wast born of woman:–
> But swords I smile at, weapons laugh to scorn,
> Brandish'd by man that's of a woman born,
>
> (V.vii.11–13)

Young Siward's death becomes in effect proof that he was born of
woman; in the logic of Macbeth's psyche, Macbeth's invulnerability
is the proof that he was not. The *but* records this fantasied
distinction: it constructs the sentence 'You, born of woman, are
vulnerable; but I, not born of woman, am not.'

In so far as this is the fantasy embodied in Macbeth at the play's end, it is punished by the equivocation of the fiends: the revelation that Macduff derives from woman, though by unusual means, musters against Macbeth all the values of ordinary family and community that Macduff carries with him. Macbeth, 'cow'd' by the revelation (V.viii.18), is forced to take on the taint of vulnerability; the fantasy of escape from the maternal matrix seems to die with him. But although this fantasy is punished in Macbeth, it does not quite die with him; it continues to have a curious life of its own in the play, apart from its embodiment in him. Even from the beginning of the play, the fantasy has not been Macbeth's alone: as the play's most striking bloody man, he is in the beginning the bearer of this fantasy for the all-male community that depends on his bloody prowess. The opening scenes strikingly construct male and female as realms apart; and the initial descriptions of Macbeth's battles construe his prowess as a consequence of his exemption from the taint of woman.

In the description of his battle with Macdonwald, what looks initially like a battle between loyal and disloyal sons to establish primacy in the father's eyes is oddly transposed into a battle of male against female:

> Doubtful it stood;
> As two spent swimmers, that do cling together
> And choke their art. The merciless Macdonwald
> (Worthy to be a rebel, for to that
> The multiplying villainies of nature
> Do swarm upon him) from the western isles
> Of Kernes and Gallowglasses is supplied;
> And Fortune, on his damned quarrel smiling,
> Show'd like a rebel's whore: but all's too weak;
> For brave Macbeth (well he deserves that name),
> Disdaining Fortune, with his brandish'd steel,
> Which smok'd with bloody execution,
> Like Valour's minion, carv'd out his passage,
> Till he fac'd the slave;
> Which ne'er shook hands, nor bade farewell to him,
> Till he unseam'd him from the nave to th' chops,
> And fix'd his head upon our battlements.
>
> (I.ii.7–23)

The two initially indistinguishable figures metaphorised as the swimmers eventually sort themselves out into victor and victim, but only by first sorting themselves out into male and female, as though Macbeth can be distinguished from Macdonwald only by making Macdonwald functionally female. The 'merciless Macdonwald' is initially firmly identified; but by the time Macbeth appears, Macdonwald has temporarily disappeared, replaced by the female figure of Fortune, against whom Macbeth seems to fight ('brave Macbeth, . . . Disdaining Fortune, with his brandish'd steel'). The metaphorical substitution of Fortune for Macdonwald transforms the battle into a contest between male and female; it makes Macbeth's deserving of his name contingent on his victory over the female. We are prepared for this transformation by Macdonwald's sexual alliance with the tainting female, the whore Fortune; Macbeth's identification as valour's minion redefines the battle as a contest between the half-female couple Fortune/Macdonwald and the all-male couple Valour/Macbeth. Metaphorically, Macdonwald and Macbeth take on the qualities of the unreliable female and the heroic male; Macbeth's battle against Fortune turns out to be his battle against Macdonwald because the two are functionally the same. Macdonwald, tainted by the female, becomes an easy mark for Macbeth, who demonstrates his own untainted manhood by unseaming Macdonwald from the nave to the chops. Through its allusions both to castration and to Caesarian section, this unseaming furthermore remakes Macdonwald's body as female, revealing what his alliance with Fortune has suggested all along.

In effect, then, the battle that supports the father's kingdom plays out the creation of a conquering all-male erotics that marks its conquest by its triumph over a feminised body, simultaneously that of Fortune and Macdonwald. Hence, in the double action of the passage, the victorious unseaming happens twice: first on the body of Fortune and then on the body of Macdonwald. The lines descriptive of Macbeth's approach to Macdonwald – 'brave Macbeth ... Disdaining Fortune, with his brandish'd steel ... carved out his passage' – make that approach contingent on Macbeth's first carving his passage through a female body, hewing his way out. The language here perfectly anticipates Macduff's birth by Caesarian section, revealed at the end of the play: if Macduff is ripped untimely from his mother's womb, Macbeth here manages in fantasy his own Caesarian section, carving his passage out from the unreliable female to achieve heroic male action, in effect carving up the female to arrive at the male. Only after this rite of passage can Macbeth meet Macdonwald: the act of aggression toward the female body, the fantasy of self-birth, marks his passage to the contest that will be definitive of his maleness partly in so far as it is definitive of Macdonwald's tainted femaleness. For the all-male community surrounding Duncan, then, Macbeth's victory is allied with his triumph over femaleness; for them, he becomes invulnerable, 'lapp'd in proof' (I.ii.55) like one of Lady Macbeth's armoured men-children. Even before his entry into the play, that is, Macbeth is the bearer of the shared fantasy that secure male community depends on the prowess of the man in effect not born of woman, the man who can carve his own passage out, the man whose very maleness is the mark of his exemption from female power.

Ostensibly, the play rejects the version of manhood implicit in the shared fantasy of the beginning. Macbeth himself is well aware that his capitulation to Lady Macbeth's definition of manhood entails his abandonment of his own more inclusive definition of what becomes a man (I.vii.46); and Macduff's response to the news of his family's destruction insists that humane feeling is central to the definition of manhood (IV.iii.221). Moreover, the revelation that even Macduff had a mother sets a limiting condition on the fantasy of a bloody masculine escape from the female and hence on the kind of manhood defined by that escape. Nonetheless, even at the end, the play enables one version of the fantasy that heroic manhood is exemption from the female even while it punishes that fantasy in Macbeth. The key figure in whom this double movement is vested in the end of the play is Macduff; the unresolved contradictions that surround him are, I think, marks of ambivalence toward the fantasy itself. In insisting that mourning for his family is his right as a man, he presents family feeling as central to the definition of manhood; and yet he conspicuously leaves his family vulnerable to destruction when he goes off to offer his services to Malcolm. The play moreover insists on reminding us that he has inexplicably abandoned his family: both Lady Macduff and Malcolm question the necessity of this abandonment (IV.ii.6–14; IV.iii.26–8); and the play never allows Macduff to explain himself. This unexplained abandonment severely qualifies Macduff's force as the play's central exemplar of a healthy manhood that can include the possibility of relationship to women: the play seems to vest diseased familial relations in Macbeth and the possibility of healthy ones in Macduff; and yet we discover dramatically that Macduff has a family only when we hear that he has abandoned it. Dramatically and psychologically, he takes on full masculine power only as he loses his family and becomes energised by the loss, converting his grief into the more 'manly' tune of vengeance (IV.iii.235); the loss of his family here enables his accession to full masculine action even while his response to that loss insists on a more humane definition of manhood. The play here pulls in two directions. It reiterates this doubleness by vesting in Macduff its final fantasy of exemption from woman. The ambivalence that shapes the portrayal of Macduff is evident even as he reveals to Macbeth that he 'was from his mother's womb / Untimely ripp'd' (V.viii.15–16): the emphasis on untimeliness and the violence of the image suggest that he has been prematurely deprived of a nurturing maternal presence; but the prophecy construes just this deprivation as the source of Macduff's strength. The prophecy itself both denies and affirms the fantasy of exemption from women: in affirming that Macduff has indeed had a mother, it denies the fantasy of male self-generation; but in attributing his power to his having been untimely ripped from that mother, it sustains the sense that violent separation from the mother is the mark of the successful male. The final battle between Macbeth and Macduff thus replays the initial battle between Macbeth and Macdonwald. But Macduff has now taken the place of Macbeth: he carries with him the male power given him by the Caesarian solution, and Macbeth is retrospectively revealed as Macdonwald, the woman's man.

The doubleness of the prophecy is less the equivocation of the fiends than Shakespeare's own equivocation about the figure of Macduff and about the fantasy vested in him in the end. For Macduff carries with him simultaneously all the values of family and the claim that masculine power derives from the unnatural abrogation of family, including escape from the conditions of one's birth. Moreover, the ambivalence that shapes the figure of Macduff similarly shapes the dramatic structure of the play itself. Ostensibly concerned to restore natural order at the end, the play bases that order upon the radical exclusion of the female. Initially construed as all-powerful, the women virtually disappear at the end, Lady Macbeth becoming so diminished a character that we scarcely trouble to ask ourselves whether the report of her suicide is accurate or not, the witches literally gone from the stage and so diminished in psychic power that Macbeth never mentions them and blames his defeat only on the equivocation of their male masters, the fiends; even Lady Macduff exists only to disappear. The bogus fulfilment of the Birnam Wood prophecy suggests the extent to which the natural order of the end depends on the exclusion of the female. Critics sometimes see in the march of Malcolm's soldiers bearing their green branches an allusion to the Maying festivals in which participants returned from the woods bearing branches, or to the ritual scourging of a hibernal figure by the forces of the oncoming spring. The allusion seems to me clearly present; but it serves, I think, to mark precisely what the moving of Birnam Wood is not. Malcolm's use of Birnam Wood is a military manoeuvre. His drily worded command (V.iv.4–7) leaves little room for suggestions of natural fertility or for the deep sense of the generative world rising up to expel its winter king; nor does the play later enable these associations except in a scattered and partly ironic way. These trees have little resemblance to those in the Forest of Arden; their branches, like those carried by the apparition of the 'child crowned, with a tree in his hand' (IV.i.86), are little more than the emblems of a strictly patriarchal family tree. This family tree, like the march of Birnam Wood itself, is relentlessly male: Duncan and sons, Banquo and son, Siward and son. There are no daughters and scarcely any mention of mothers in these family trees. We are brought as close as possible here to the fantasy of family without women. In that sense, Birnam Wood is the perfect emblem of the nature that triumphs at the end of the play: nature without generative possibility, nature without women. Malcolm tells his men to carry the branches to obscure themselves, and that is exactly their function: in so far as they seem to allude to the rising of the natural order against Macbeth, they obscure the operations of male power, disguising them as a natural force; and they simultaneously obscure the extent to which natural order itself is here reconceived as purely male.

If we can see the fantasy of escape from the female in the play's fulfilment of the witches' prophecies – in Macduff's birth by Caesarian section and in Malcolm's appropriation of Birnam Wood – we can see it also in the play's psychological geography. The shift from Scotland to England is strikingly the shift from the mother's to the father's terrain. Scotland 'cannot / Be call'd our mother, but our grave' (IV.iii.165–6), in Rosse's words to Macduff: it is the realm of Lady Macbeth and the witches, the realm in which the mother *is* the grave, the realm appropriately ruled by their bad son Macbeth. The escape to England is an escape from their power into the realm of the good father-king and his surrogate son Malcolm, 'unknown to woman' (IV.iii.126). The magical power of this father to cure clearly balances the magical power of the witches to harm, as Malcolm (the father's son) balances Macbeth (the mother's son). That Macduff can cross from one realm into the other only by abandoning his family suggests the rigidity of the psychic geography separating England from Scotland. At the end of the play, Malcolm returns to Scotland mantled in the power England gives him, in effect bringing the power of the fathers with him: bearer of his father's line, unknown to woman, supported by his agent Macduff (empowered by his own special immunity from birth), Malcolm embodies utter separation from women and as such triumphs easily over Macbeth, the mother's son.

The play that begins by unleashing the terrible threat of destructive maternal power and demonstrates the helplessness of its central male figure before that power thus ends by consolidating male power, in effect solving the problem of masculinity by eliminating the female. In the psychological fantasies that I am tracing, the play portrays the failure of the androgynous parent to protect his son, that son's consequent fall into the dominion of the bad mothers, and the final victory of a masculine order in which mothers no longer threaten because they no longer exist. In that sense, *Macbeth* is a recuperative consolidation of male power, a consolidation in the face of the threat unleashed in *Hamlet* and especially in *King Lear* and never fully contained in those plays. In *Macbeth*, maternal power is given its most virulent sway and then abolished; at the end of the play we are in a purely male realm. We will not be in so absolute a male realm again until we are in Prospero's island-kingdom, similarly based firmly on the exiling of the witch Sycorax.

From *Cannibals, Witches, and Divorce: Estranging the Renaissance*, ed. Marjorie Garber (Baltimore and London, 1987), pp. 93–4, 100–11.

NOTES

[Some psychoanalytic criticism of Shakespeare has been criticised by feminists and materialists for suggesting that there is one essential, normative kind of human development towards 'maturity'; or, rather, two kinds: one for boy children and one for girl children. However, Janet Adelman's essay needs only the universal proposition that males are born from women: this is the basis for the anxiety which she locates in *Macbeth*. The essay has been shortened for this reprinting; also, there has not been space to include the substantial notes in which Professor Adelman discusses a range of further psychoanalytic criticism. *Macbeth* is quoted from the New Arden edition, ed. Kenneth Muir (London, 1972). Ed.]

1. See Muir, New Arden edition, note to I.v.48.

6

Imperfect Speakers: the Tale Thickens

MALCOLM EVANS

At the end of his first encounter with the 'weyward sisters', Macbeth addresses them as 'imperfect Speakers' (I.iii.170) and bids them to tell him more. On the order 'Speake, I charge you' (179), they disappear like bubbles into the earth, leaving Macbeth and Banquo to doubt their own perceptions, and their language. When Banquo asks if they have 'eaten on the insane Root', he also wonders about the reality of 'such things . . . as we doe *speake* about' (185–6). The tentative moves of Macbeth and Banquo to verbally grasp what has happened are like an old song, a nursery game which recalls the doggerel of the sisters themselves:

> **Macbeth**   Your Children shall be Kings
> **Banquo**   You shall be King
> **Macbeth**   And *Thane* of Cawdor too: wente it not
>   so?
> **Banquo**   To th' selfe-same tune, and words:
> (I.iii.188–91)

When Rosse, at this point, enters to deliver his report, it is clear that 'imperfect speaking' is not a disorder exclusive to the sisters or to those who have been in immediate contact with them:

> The King hath happily receiv'd, *Macbeth*,
> The newes of thy successe: and when he reades
> Thy personall Venture in the Rebels fight,
> His Wonders and his Prayses do contend,

Which should be thine, or his: silenc'd with
  that,
In viewing o're the rest o' th' selfe-same day,
He findes thee in the stout Norweyan Rankes,
Nothing afeard of what thy selfe didst make
Strange Images of death, as thick as Tale
Can post with post, and every one did beare
Thy prayses in his Kingdomes great defence,
And powr'd them downe before him.

                                        (I.iii. 193–204)

The perplexing density of Rosse's report releases imperfections of its own, while repeating the haste and excitement of the messengers and narratives it describes, which arrive headlong and inarticulate, 'as thick as Tale / Can post with post', leaving Duncan amazed, silent, and finally awash in information. The thickening of Rosse's account is a contagion caught from these other reports or an indication, perhaps, of his own penchant for the 'Relation too nice' (IV.iii.2010) later criticised by Macduff. There is a call here for a performance which incorporates at once a lack and an excess of rhetorical preparation, and the information imparted reproduces this uneasy play of opposites. Verbal and syntactic ambiguities edge the heroic image of Macbeth from the good to the evil cause – 'Thy personall venture in the Rebels fight', 'He findes thee in the stout Norweyan Rankes'. This shifting also applies to Duncan, drawn into the narrative to the extent of occupying its protagonist's position. 'When he reades', the king becomes his subject, Macbeth, mirroring in the contention of 'Which should be thine, or his' the usurpation that is imminent. The tale thickens further as Macbeth becomes not only protagonist but author, of 'Strange Images of death', and reader, in place of the king, of Rosse's narrative about narratives.

Any attempt to relate the content of narratives in the early scenes of *Macbeth* has to negotiate a conflict between two basic linguistic modes which results in a potentially baffling opacity. On the one side is the attempt to construct an unequivocal idiom in which the theory of the divine right of kings and its place in the Great Chain of Being is made one with nature to the extent that the 'unnatural', constitutive operations of language itself are strenuously deleted. On the other there is an inescapable undertow of negation, in which the hurly-burly of language which precedes the construction of these sealed hierarchical categories leaks back to interrupt the 'natural' quality their linguistic mode silently claims for itself. In Rosse's speech the first mode, affirming a positive metaphysical 'order' which can somehow, magically, exist outside language and ideology, appears in the attempt to conjure up a grateful, generous king and his loyal, heroic subject. Its negation is the intractability of language, which intimates a more deeply rooted disorder than the one that has just been quelled, and a potentially unending circulation of subjects through hierarchical positions that only *seem* to be fixed and sovereign – of king and thane, of author, reader and protagonist.

The same 'thickening' of the tale and dispersal of clear ideological categories divides the language of the 'bleeding Captaine' at the beginning of the play. The captain's report of the battle opens with a reference to the 'choked Art' of spent swimmers who cling together for support and ends with the choking of his own voice and the cacophony of gashes that 'cry for helpe' (I.ii.63). The Arden editor argues that, under these circumstances, some incoherence might be expected[1] but the form it takes is no different from that in Rosse's tale. First there is the intention of affirming an ideal of manhood and service validated by reference to natural hierarchies and centred on Banquo and Macbeth, whom the rebels can dismay no more than 'Sparrowes, Eagles / Or the Hare the Lyon' (54–5). But the language of the narrative palters 'in a double sence' no less than that of the play's central and most conscious 'imperfect Speakers', the sisters, incorporating their characteristic blend of confusion and prophecy. The rebels, by the end of the speech, have been compared implicitly with the crucified Christ, and Macbeth and Banquo with his torturers (60–1). In the interim, the narrative production of a 'brave *Macbeth* (well hee deserves that Name)' (35) has already been thrown into crisis, if not by a graphic excess in the description of 'legitimate' violence then at least by strategic ambiguities in the text. Seeking the rebel Macdonwald, Macbeth:

> Disdayning Fortune, with his brandisht steele,
> Which smoak'd with bloody execution
> (Like Valours Minion) carv'd out his passage,
> Till hee fac'd the Slave:
> Which nev'r shooke hands, nor bade farewell to him,
> Till he unseam'd him from the Nave to th' Chops,
> And fix'd his Head upon our Battlements.
>
> (I.ii. 36–42)

The clause 'Which nev'r shooke hands ...', applying equally, and in different senses, to Fortune, Macbeth, or the Slave, disturbs the balance of a complex syntactic structure, which totters to the climactic image of an impaled rebellious head, Macdonwald's but also, proleptically, already that of Macbeth, his own worst enemy.

Such instances of disruption to the harmonious, univocal discourse of Tudor and Stuart absolutism proliferate in the early scenes of *Macbeth*. Rosse's first report to the king anticipates some of the instabilities of his language when he later addresses Macbeth and Banquo. Here another ambiguous 'Macbeth' faces the treacherous thane of Cawdor, a title soon to be his own, confronting him 'with selfe-comparisons, / Point against Point, rebellious Arme 'gainst Arme' (I.ii.80–1). Again too much, and too little, is stated with the result that the image of the defender of right merges into its opposite. Equivocation in these opening scenes is a condition of language, which moves constantly back from the articulated code to an anterior heterogeneity, melting, like the sisters after their encounter with Macbeth and Banquo, 'as breath into the Winde' (I.iii.183). Macbeth's first words in the play, 'So foule and faire a day I have not seene' (I.iii.137), establish his connection with the sisters before they have even met. But the motion of their 'faire is foul, and foule is fair' (I.i.12), which L. C. Knights described as a 'metaphysical pitch-and-toss',[2] extends not only to those who become directly implicated in what the language of metaphysics would describe as 'evil'. Even Duncan, the perfect, saintly king of *Macbeth* criticism, unintentionally equivocates himself into complicity with his own downfall, confusion's masterpiece, when he acknowledges to his general, 'More is thy due than more than all can pay' (I.iv.304).

The crisis of the sign and unequivocal discourse in the play is paralleled by that of the unified subject. As Macbeth embarks on the passage from 'Glamis' to 'Cawdor' to 'King', the identity sustained in the hierarchical order is fractured. After the first meeting with the sisters, when the prospect of murder is still only 'fantasticall', the thought still 'Shakes so my single state of Man / That function is smother'd in surmise' (I.iii.252–3). By finally daring to do more than 'may become a man' (I.vii.525), he ceases to be a coherent subject, either of Duncan or in the sense of an intact, self-present identity. *Macbeth*, as Catherine Belsey has pointed out, explores the relationship between crisis in the 'state', or the social order, and disruption in the 'single state' of the subject.[3] Once the structures of Duncan's kingdom are wrenched from their place in 'nature', Macbeth himself becomes a plurality, a process rather than a fixity. In the same movement the bonds between the state, the subject and the unequivocal linguistic mode of 'order' and 'nature', always suspended in 'imperfect speaking', are broken. Only the 'weyward sisters' who inhabit the heath, outside the closures of the social formation, can properly perform 'A deed without a name' (IV.i.1579). But after Duncan's murder Macduff can speak of a 'horror' which 'Tongue nor Heart cannot conceive, nor name' (II.iii.816–17), while Macbeth recognises that 'To know my deed, / 'Twere best not know my selfe' (II.i.737–8). The semantic volatility of all the earlier narratives, the negative undertow which compromises the ordered, 'natural' discourse of ideology and its unified subjects, finally comes into its own in the 'written troubles of the Braine' (V.iii.2264) that emanate from Lady Macbeth betwen sleep and waking, madness and reason, and, most crucially, in Macbeth's description of life as 'a Tale / Told by an Ideot, full of sound and fury / Signifying nothing' (V.v.2347–9). The 'nothing' signified is not merely an absence but a delirious plenitude of selves and meanings, always prior to, and in excess of, the self-naturalising signs and subjects of the discourses it calls perpetually to account.

The Macbeths, with the sisters, spill over the limits of 'character' to constitute the text's 'nothing' which, in turn, constantly erodes and undermines the hierarchies of irreducible 'somethings' proposed by metaphysics. To define this space of 'nothing' quite simply as 'evil' is to reprocess the text through a moral discourse it renders problematic. Even in orthodox Christian doctrine, if 'nothing' is identifiable with sin or chaos it is also the ground of all creation, and *Macbeth* also signifies nothing in this paradoxically positive sense. The unequivocal discourse of a metaphysically sanctioned absolutism, even when it succeeds in avoiding self-contradiction and the interpenetration of opposites is 'single' not only in the sense of 'unified' or 'unambiguous' but also in a second sense, exploited here as in other plays, of 'weak' or 'simple-minded'.[4] In the choric scene following the murder of Duncan, Rosse and the Old Man discuss the night which has 'trifled former knowings' (II.iv.928) in terms that permit these 'former knowings' to reassert themselves with a vengeance.

The studied theatrical archaism of the scene sets off the credulous rhetoric of Rosse and the geriatric amazement of his interlocutor, who together reconstitute order in a reprise of the bloody Captain's bird and animal lore. The feudal norm is unequivocally reaffirmed in the outrage of Duncan's horses breaking from their stalls and proceeding to 'eate each other', a fact the Old Man prefaces with the standard formula for this type of narrative, ''Tis said . . .' (945). The same system of 'natural' correspondences is at work in his image of a falcon, 'by a Mowsing Owle hawkt at, and kill'd' (939), but the 'singleness' of this type of language always sits uneasily in the text. It marks the language of Duncan and Banquo when they first arrive at Macbeth's castle, hallowed in their minds by the presence of the birds who make each 'Jutty frieze', 'buttrice' and 'Coigne of Vantage' the place for a 'pendant bed, and procreant Cradle, / Where they must breed, and haunt' (I.vi.439–42). There is clearly a hint here of the 'life-themes' discovered by G. Wilson Knight,[5] but the situational ironies also tend to strip the rhetoric away from its experiential and 'natural' base, revealing that the birds at least, if not Banquo and Duncan, are a little naïve in their literal adherence to the 'Elizabethan World Picture'. There is a similar element of bathos in Macduff's first reaction to the murder of his 'pretty chickens, and their Damme' by the 'Hell-Kite' Macbeth (IV.iii.2066–7), particularly in the context of his desertion of his family. After his father's flight, in response to the question 'How will you live?', the young Macduff replies 'As Birds do, Mother' (IV.ii.1747–8), an answer in which echoes of the Shakespearean fool mark a limit to the pretensions of one of the text's most insistent images of 'order' – 'Let them eat ideology'.

The choric exchange between Rosse and the Old Man ends, after the play's most sustained burst of 'singleness', with a benediction which is also a curse and which restores to the text its characteristic signification of 'nothing'. As he leaves, the Old Man bids 'Gods benyson go with you, and with those / That would make good of bad, and Friends of Foes' (II.iv.1978–9). His blessing applies equally to those who speak of falcons, owls, eagles and sparrows and to the proponents of 'faire is foule, and foule is faire' who bring, from the viewpoint of the bird-watchers, a curse to Scotland. No one makes 'good of bad' more forcefully than the Macbeths, who harness the ambiguities of language in the process. Lady Macbeth, for whom the 'single' is the inadequate, courts 'doubleness' in its various senses. In response to Duncan's pedantic greeting to 'our honor'd Hostesse', she affirms:

> All our service
> In every point twice done, and then done
>   double,
> Were poore, and single Businesse to contend
> Against those Honors deepe, and broad,
> Wherewith your Majestie loades our house
>
> (I.vi.449–53)

The 'Honors' here connote titles already bestowed on Macbeth, the royal presence which now graces his castle, and the sinister opportunities for further advancement that presence affords. The service done 'double' implies not only the obvious numerical sense but also the involvement of 'strength' and 'duplicity'. Making good out of bad is, at one level, a definition of this type of hypocritical show, in which the sense directed to the naïve 'single' hearer is enriched by the speaker's recognition of true intentions. In the case of Macbeth, his 'single state' broken open, one utterance may disclose different levels of duplicity and delusion in the process of the same subject. When Duncan's murder is revealed, he announces:

> Had I but dy'd an houre before this chance,
> I had liv'd a blessed time: for from this instant,
> There's nothing serious in Mortalitie:
> All is but Toyes:
>
> (II.iii.852–5)

While the regicide conceals his crime beneath an extravagant show of 'single' piety, unknown to him the Macbeth of 'Tomorrow, and tomorrow, and tomorrow' is already, by indirection, speaking an unequivocal truth.

In summary, the density of the narratives that accumulate in the early scenes of *Macbeth* is produced by a conflict between two linguistic modes. The first, which attempts to suppress the constitutive role of language, is the 'single', unequivocal identification of the ideology of divine right with nature. It pertains, in its own terms, to the 'good characters' of the play and the birds. The second, most fully itself in the language of the sisters and the protagonists, is evident elsewhere whenever 'imperfect speaking' cuts into the first mode and restores to it a discordant element of linguistic materiality and heterogeneity. The two modes proceed side by side until the end of the play, never fully resolving themselves into a unity. When Malcolm finally assumes power, the restoration of 'single' discourse is announced in his description of the Macbeths as 'this dead Butcher, and his Fiend-like Queene' (V.vii.2522), the most reductive and parsimonious of all possible definitions, the mark of a speaker whose sole foray into equivocation, in the testing of Macduff in Act 4, scene 3, lacks altogether the Vice's theatrical panache inherited by his antagonist. In contrast to Macbeth's, his discourse 'knows' and 'sees' very little or, to put it another way, does not know 'nothing'. Malcolm's 'single state' is ripe for an encounter with the sisters.

There is an influential strand in *Macbeth* criticism, one particularly suited in the recent past to the practical exegetical requirements of students, which works with the text's unequivocal mode to deliver a clear account of it as a 'morality play', a 'vision of evil', a 'statement of evil', or 'the story of a noble and valiant man who is brought to his damnation, presented in such a way as to arouse our pity and terror'.[6] The pandemic 'pitch-and-toss' and 'imperfect speaking' which unseat metaphysics in the play clearly fail to reach out to the critical discourse which can so casually refurbish 'morality', 'evil' and 'damnation'. At heart this is still the 'Shakespeare' of the Reverend Sims, embellished with images, themes, characters and a story but directed to the statement of a central, transcendent 'truth' in the text.[7] These secondary narratives, which purport to help the text along in delivering its essential meanings, do so by privileging, at their most fundamental level, its 'single' mode and ignoring, or banishing to the realms of 'evil' or 'exquisite complexity', the 'unnatural' operations of language that divide and 'thicken' narrative in the play itself, which is ultimately no more an affirmation of metaphysical unity and order than a contradictory 'Tale / Told by an Ideot, full of sound and fury / Signifying nothing'.

Antonin Artaud regarded Shakespeare as the source of 400 years of dramatic 'falsehood and illusion', of a 'purely descriptive and narrative theatre – storytelling psychology' in which the stage is kept separate from the audience, and administers to its public the dominant cultural and ideological forms. This may be true of the 'single' *Macbeth* sustained by much modern criticism and theatrical production but not of the other play which, by fissuring the 'natural' subjects and signs that exist for and in ideology, achieves precisely what Artaud denies: a 'Shakespeare' who leaves his audience intact 'without setting off one image that will shake the organism to its foundations and leave an ineffaceable scar'.[8] But this latter play has much to contend with, quite apart from the critical assumptions that transform ideology into 'human values' and recover from the Shakespearean text, however complex, their suitably harmonious vehicle. A normative criticism will always affirm unity by marginalising texts, or parts of texts, where 'Shakespeare' is nodding or not speaking perfectly. The Newbolt Report advised teachers to avoid passages which were not 'verbally inspired'; for example, 'the tediously protracted dialogue' between Malcolm and Macduff in Act 4, scene 3, of *Macbeth*[9] – a point where the 'singleness' of text and criticism is most at risk. Where pedagogic or discursive exclusion is impossible, another available strategy is the theoretical splits, guaranteed to unseam any commentator from nave to chops. So Kenneth Muir wishes away the contradictory thickening of the bloody Captain's tale by combining naturalism – the wounded man is exhausted and therefore incoherent – with an extreme of conventional formalism in which the character 'utters bombastic language, not because he is himself bombastic, but because such language was considered appropriate to epic narration'.[10] Fair is foul and foul is fair, and in the last instance the text can be recovered from its own imperfect speaking by forms of rewriting and incrustation not dreamed of even in Macherey's philosophy.[11] In nearly all modern editions, Rosse's description of the messages that reach Duncan 'as thick as Tale / Can post with post' – words 'well within the normal language patterns of this time'[12] – has been excised. Rosse now delivers lines written by Nicholas Rowe in 1709, in which reports 'As thick as *hail, / Came* post with post'. And what could be more natural?

From Malcolm Evans, *Signifying Nothing: Truth's True Contents in Shakespeare's Text* (Brighton, 1986), pp. 113–22.

NOTES

[Malcolm Evans's concern is with a poststructuralist analysis of how language and culture work – consider the title of his book, above. As with Terry Eagleton's piece (essay 4), distrust of the authority of writing releases a witty and teasing kind of critical prose. *Macbeth* is quoted from *The Norton Facsimile: The First Folio of Shakespeare*, ed. C. Hinman (New York, 1968); observe that this is a deliberate choice by Evans: we cannot take 'the text' for granted. Ed.]

1. Kenneth Muir (ed.), *Macbeth*, New Arden edition (London, 1953, 8th edn), note to I.ii.42–3.

2. L. C. Knights, *Explorations* (London, 1946), p. 18.

3. Catherine Belsey, *Critical Practice* (London, 1980), pp. 89–90.

4. Shakespeare, *Romeo and Juliet*, 1169; *2 Henry IV*, I.ii.444.

5. G. Wilson Knight, *The Imperial Theme* (London, 1951), p. 125f.

6. W. Farnham, *Shakespeare's Tragic Frontier* (Berkeley, 1950), p. 79; G. W. Knight, *The Wheel of Fire*, 4th edn (London, 1949), p. 140; Knights, *Explorations*, p. 18; Muir (ed.), *Macbeth*, p. lv.

7. A. E. Sims, *A Shakespeare Birthday Book* (London, n.d.) – [described by

Evans on pp. 101–2 of his book as comprising '365 eternal verities and moral injunctions culled from the plays and poems'. Ed.]

8. Antonin Artaud, *The Theater and Its Double*, trans. M. C. Richards (New York, 1958), pp. 76–7.

9. Sir Henry Newbolt, *The Teaching of English in England*, Board of Education (London, 1921), p. 314.

10. Muir (ed.), *Macbeth*, pp. li, 88.

11. See 'An Interview with Pierre Macherey', ed. C. Mercer and J. Radford, *Red Letters*, 55 (1977), 3–9.

12. Hilda M. Hulme, *Explorations in Shakespeare's Language* (London, 1962), p. 25.

7

Subjectivity and the Soliloquy

CATHERINE BELSEY

... The common feature of liberal humanism, justifying the use of the single phrase, is a commitment to *man*, whose essence is *freedom*. Liberal humanism proposes that the subject is the free, unconstrained author of meaning and action, the origin of history. Unified, knowing and autonomous, the human being seeks a political system which guarantees freedom of choice. Western liberal democracy, humanism claims, freely chosen, and thus evidently the unconstrained expression of human nature, was born in the seventeenth century with the emergence of the individual and the victory of constitutionalism in the consecutive English revolutions of the 1640s and 1688. But in the century since these views were established as self-evident, doubts have arisen concerning this reading of the past as the triumphant march of progress towards the moment when history levels off into the present. And from the new perspectives which have given rise to these doubts, both liberal humanism and the subject it produces appear to be an effect of a continuing history, rather than its culmination. The individual, it now seems, was not after all released at last from the heads of people who had waited only for the peace and leisure to cultivate what lay ineluctably within them and within all of us. On the contrary, the liberal-humanist subject, the product of a specific epoch and a specific class, was constructed in conflict and in contradiction – with conflicting and contradictory consequences.

One of these contradictions is the inequality of freedom. While in theory all *men* are equal, men and women are not symmetrically defined. Man, the centre and hero of liberal humanism, was produced in contradistinction to the objects of his knowledge, and in terms of the relations of power in the economy and the state. Woman was produced in contradistinction to man, and in terms of the relations of power in the family. Woman's story in the sixteenth and seventeenth centuries lags behind man's. The field of women's resistance, however, is more sharply defined. ...

Liberal humanism, locating agency and meaning in the unified human subject, becomes an orthodoxy at the moment when the bourgeoisie is installed as the ruling class. Signifying practice, however, is not so well ordered as to wait for the execution of Charles I in 1649 before proclaiming the existence of an interiority, the inalienable and unalterable property of the individual, which precedes and determines speech and action. Here, for instance, is Daniel Rogers in 1642 on the grounds of marriage:

> Its true generally, but in this point specially, that speech is the discoverer of the mind: looke what the abundance of the heart is, that will vent it selfe at the mouth.... Yea, the speech of each to other should bee (without flattery) as the glasse to behold each other in.[1]

And in 1643 Milton identifies as the main grounds for divorce,

> that indisposition, unfitness, or contrariety of mind, arising from a cause in nature unchangable, hindring and ever likely to hinder the main benefits of conjugal society, which are solace and peace.[2]

In each case the subject is understood to be both single and stable, and thus synchronically and diachronically continuous where Mankind is discontinuous. Subjectivity manifests itself in speech and behaviour, making for compatibility or incompatibility between two given dispositions. Brathwait, writing in 1630, asserts even more firmly the diachronic continuity of the subject. People may seem to change, he insists, but this is simply a matter of appearances, like clouds covering the sun. In time people's true dispositions emerge and these are unalterable, 'being so inherent in the subject, as they may be moved, but not removed'. They are not affected by circumstances. External conditions have no influence on the nature of the individual. 'Shouldst thou change aire, and soile, and all, it were not in thy power to change thy selfe'.[3]

Milton and Rogers identify this fixed self with the mind, a space hollowed out by discourse within each person and then filled with a unified and unchanging essence. 'The mind is its own place', as Satan was later to assure his troops, though he perhaps rather overestimated its powers in what followed: 'and in itself / Can make a heaven of hell, a hell of heaven'.[4] This interiority, this consciousness which is also being, defines the humanist subject, the author and origin of meaning and choice. ...

THE SOLILOQUY

How is the impression of interiority produced? Above all by means of the formal development of the soliloquy. The soliloquy, as Raymond Williams has pointed out, is the condition of the possibility of presenting on the stage a new conception of the free-standing individual.[5] In conjunction with the more or less contemporaneous development of the iambic pentameter, the soliloquy makes audible the personal voice and offers access to the presence of an individual speaker. In contrast to the alliterative verse of the fifteenth century, and the 'tumbling' fourteeners characteristic of the sixteenth-century moralities, the more flexible and fluent iambic pentameter, to the degree that it does not rhyme and is not necessarily end-stopped, disavows the materiality of the process of enunciation and simulates a voice expressing the self 'behind' the speech.[6] As the literal drama discards allegory, and morality personifications give way to social types, concrete individuals, the moral conflicts externalised in the moralities are internalised in the soliloquy and thus understood to be confined *within* the *mind* of the protagonist. The struggle between good and evil shifts its centre from the macrocosm to the microcosm.

In *Doctor Faustus* (1592?), for example, in spite of the play's obvious formal and thematic continuities with the morality tradition, the hero is predominantly a free-standing, literal figure in a geographically- and chronologically-specific world. Faustus first appears alone in his study, and though later Mephostophilis claims to have turned the pages of the Bible to lead him to the false syllogism,[7] the text gives no evidence that he is visible to the audience at this point. On the contrary, Faustus is apparently alone, and it is in soliloquy that he makes his decision to seek a deity. When the Good and Bad Angels appear and address him, Faustus gives no indication that he has heard them. They appear in response to the doubts formulated by Faustus himself: unlike the corresponding figures in *The Castle of Perseverance*, they do not initiate the moral debates. In an ironic reversal of the morality tradition, Faustus summons his own destroyer, and it is Mephostophilis who pleads with him to renounce his unlawful demands (ll.309–10). The abstractions, in other words, have become relatively peripheral. The Angels are shadowy figures whose very existence might be an illusion. Mephostophilis, despite his denial, could be the product of a conjuring trick (ll.273–82). The shrunken personifications and the pliant Vice are diminished in proportion to the dominance of a human hero whose conflict is largely internalised.

But the Renaissance soliloquy shows evidence of its own genealogy, rendering precarious precisely the unified subjectivity which it is its project to represent. The repressed discontinuities of the allegorical tradition return to haunt the single voice which speaks. In the struggle between resolution and remorse which structures the soliloquies of Faustus the distinct voices of the allegorical tradition are clearly audible. In the following instance, though Faustus is alone and the speech is formally a soliloquy, it is as if the Bad Angel addresses him – by name and in the second person – while Faustus, like Mankind a century and a half before, hesitates, hearing the voice of the Good Angel urge him in the opposite direction. I give the soliloquy with the 'voice' of the Bad Angel in italics to show the effect of dialogue:

> *Now Faustus, must thou needs be damn'd,*
> *And canst not now be sav'd.*
> *What bootes it then to thinke on God or Heaven?*
> *Away with such vaine fancies, and despaire,*
> *Despair in GOD, and trust in Belzebub:*
> *Now go not backward: no, Faustus, be resolute:*
> *Why waverst thou?* O something soundeth in mine eares,
> Abjure this Magicke, turne to God againe.
> I and Faustus will turne to God againe.
> *To God? he loves thee not . . .*
>
> (ll.389–98)

The 'voice' of the Bad Angel combines reasoning, coaxing and imperatives, like the traditional Vice. Meanwhile the 'voice' of the Good Angel sounds in his ears and Faustus responds. The three figures of the traditional morality debate have clearly differentiated roles within this soliloquy.

The final speech of the play is an internalised psychomachia between despair and repentance, the certainty of death and a longing to escape. Its closest analogue in the moralities is the dialogue between Death and Everyman (*Everyman, c.*1500).[8] Everyman's terror mounts gradually. He begs at first for twelve years to repent, and later pleads, 'Spare me till tomorrow'. Eventually he learns the meaning of death: it is eternal, irrevocable, solitary. Everyman turns to flee, but in vain. Death's repeated 'nay' is stern and implacable, preventing all escape. Finally Everyman comes close to despair, wishing he had never been born. In Faustus's last soliloquy two voices are also distinguishable, one cold, rational, certain, the other pleading and bargaining like Everyman. I give a section of the speech with the voice of Death in italics. Here the unease of the formal disjunction between unity and discontinuity is evident in the fact that Death identifies Faustus now in the second person, now in the third, and once in the first person:

> *Ah Faustus,*
> *Now hast thou but one bare houre to live,*
> *And then thou must be damn'd perpetually.*
> Stand still you ever moving Spheares of heaven,
> That time may cease, and midnight never come;
> Faire natures eye, rise, rise againe and make
> Perpetuall day: or let this houre be but
> A yeare, a month, a weeke, a naturall day,
> That Faustus may repent, and save his soule.
> O lente lente currite noctis equi:
> *The stars move still, time runs, the clocke will strike,*
> *The devill will come, and Faustus must be damn'd.*
> O, Ile leape up to my God: who pulls me downe?
> See see where Christs bloud streames in the firmament,
> One drop would save my soule, halfe a drop, ah my Christ.
> Rend not my heart, for naming of my Christ,
> Yet I will call on him: O, spare me Lucifer.
> Where is it now? 'tis gone. *And see where God*
> *Stretcheth out his arme and bends his irefull browes*:
> Mountaines and hils, come, come and fall on me,
> And hide me from the heavy wrath of God.
> *No,* no?
> Then will I headlong run into the earth:
> Gape earth; *O no it will not harbour me.*
>
> (ll.1926–48)

Who, then, is speaking, when Faustus speaks of – or to, or about – himself? The speaker, the subject of the enunciation, is there before us on the stage, palpably a unity. But the subject of the utterance, the subject inscribed in the speech, is fragmented, discontinuous. In a similar way Hieronimo in soliloquy in *The Spanish Tragedy* (*c*.1590) is at once unified and discontinuous.[9] Hieronimo cites to himself the scriptural prohibition on human revenge, 'Vindicta mihi', and replies to himself. 'Ay, heaven will be reveng'd of every ill.' And then in the imperative, 'Then stay, Hieronimo.' But in another and contradictory imperative, 'Strike, and strike home, where wrong is offered thee'. Six lines in the second person lead to resolution in the first: 'And to conclude, I will revenge his death'. There follow eighteen lines defining in the first person a strategy for avoiding detection and then, the choice of action settled, an imperative addressed to himself to assemble in a single cause the fragments which constitute the human being:

> Hieronimo, thou must enjoin
> Thine eyes to observation, and thy tongue
> To milder speeches than thy spirit affords,
> Thy heart to patience, and thy hands to rest,
> Thy cap to courtesy, and thy knee to bow,
> Till to revenge thou know, when, where and how.

In the tradition of the psychomachia the fragments of being are predominantly abstract moral or psychological qualities, but the distinction between physical and psychological properties is a modern one – the effect of the humanist isolation of the mind as the essence of the subject. In the 'little world made cunningly / Of elements', where the blend of humours defines disposition, the physical and the psychological are continuous. The repentant Everyman greets his own Beauty, Strength and Five Senses, as well as Discretion and Knowledge, only to be parted from them all as he crawls into the grave. Lady Macbeth's invocation to cruelty displays the contradictory nature of the subject in the early seventeenth century:

> Come, you spirits
> That tend on mortal thoughts, unsex me here;
> And fill me, from the crown to the toe, top-full
> Of direst cruelty. Make thick my blood,
> Stop up th' access and passage to remorse,
> That no compunctious visitings of nature
> Shake my fell purpose nor keep peace between
> Th' effect and it. Come to my woman's breasts
> And take my milk for gall, you murd'ring ministers,
> Wherever in your sightless substances

You wait on nature's mischief. Come, thick night,
And pall thee in the dunnest smoke of hell,
That my keen knife see not the wound it makes,
Nor heaven peep through the blanket of the dark
To cry 'Hold, hold'.

(*Macbeth*, I.v.37–51)

The speaker, Lady Macbeth, the subject of the enunciation, is visible on the stage, there before us as a unity, performing the invocation. But the subject of the utterance is barely present in the speech. It is not the grammatical subject of the actions – the spirits are – and the moment it appears (as 'me') in the third line of the text, it is divided into crown, toe, cruelty, blood, remorse, nature, breasts, milk. The speech concludes with the opposition between heaven and hell, reproducing the morality pattern of the human being as a battle-ground between cosmic forces, autonomous only to the point of choosing between them.

The contradictions between unity and discontinuity produce, from a humanist point of view, some odd effects. When Sir Charles Mountford in *A Woman Killed with Kindness* (1603) kills two men in a fight, he exclaims:

My God! what have I done? what have I done?
My rage hath plung'd into a sea of blood.
In which my soul lies drown'd.

Remorse is instantaneous and induces what sounds to a modern interpretation suspiciously like equivocation: 'It was not I, but rage, did this vile murder'. But the line that follows makes it clear that the isolation of rage is not an evasion of the consequences: 'Yet I, and not my rage, must answer it'.[10] The episode is parallel in some ways to the end of *Othello*, where Othello the Venetian executes Othello the pagan in the name of Venetian justice (V.ii.341–59).

Leavis, from a humanist perspective, reads Othello's final speech as 'un-self-comprehending' 'self-dramatisation'.[11] This assumes, of course, not only a self to be comprehended and dramatised, but also an anterior self to do the dramatising and comprehending (or not). What makes such a reading not only possible but persuasive? The answer, again, is that it is above all an effect of the formal development of the soliloquy. The precariously unified protagonist of Renaissance drama is in practice marked by another division which points forwards to a fully-fledged humanism rather than backwards to the Middle Ages, and this is the source of the subject's imaginary interiority. Even, or indeed perhaps especially, when the soliloquy is all in the first person, when the subject defined there is continuous and non-fragmentary, the occurrence of 'I' in speech is predicated on a gap between the subject of the enunciation and the subject of the utterance, the subject who is defined in the speech. Since the subject of the enunciation always exceeds the subject of the utterance, the 'I' cannot be fully present in what it says of itself. It is this gap which opens the possibility of glimpsing an identity behind what is said, a silent self anterior to the utterance, 'that within which passes show'. The project of humanist criticism is to fill this gap.

The gap is inevitable; whether we set out to fill it is a matter of choice. In his opening speech in *The Castle of Perseverance* the newborn Mankind defines his own helplessness: 'I not wedyr to gon ne to lende / To helpe myself mydday nyn morn'.[12] He goes on to define his predicament. Like everyone else he has two angels, one who comes from Christ and the other who is his inveterate enemy and will lead him to hell (ll.301–9). If we attend primarily to the state of mind of the speaker, the subject of the enunciation, the speech is absurd. No baby knows these things. And if Mankind knows them he is not as helpless as he pretends. The precocious infant is evidently seeking attention and is probably prone to paranoia. In this he bears some resemblance to Leavis's Othello. But of course in this instance we do not read the text in this way. To make sense of *The Castle of Perseverance* is to identify Mankind with the figure defined *in* the speech, ignorant of the world, torn between conflicting imperatives, possessing some knowledge and a great deal of uncertainty. It is to read the speech primarily as information for the audience about what a human being is, rather than as access to a personal consciousness at a particular moment. In other words, it is to focus on the subject of the utterance and not on the subject of the enunciation.

But when the fragments are internalised the gap between the two subjects is prised open in a way which seems to invite a different kind of reading. Where is the focus of the audience's attention when Wendoll in *A Woman Killed with Kindness* struggles to resist his desire for Anne Frankford, wife of his friend and benefactor?

> I am a villain if I apprehend
> But such a thought; then to attempt the deed –

Slave, thou art damn'd without redemption.
I'll drive away this passion with a song.
A song! Ha, ha! A song, as if, fond man,
Thy eyes could swim in laughter, when thy soul
Lies drench'd and drowned in red tears of blood.
I'll pray, and see if God within my heart,
Plant better thoughts. Why, prayers are meditations,
And when I meditate – O God, forgive me –
It is on her divine perfections.

                                        (VI.1–11)

Who is speaking here? A villain? No, because the speaker repudiates
this villain as damned, as foolish. The villain becomes 'thou' –
precisely not the speaker. A virtuous man, then? No, because the
figure defined in the speech cannot pray but only submit to his own
desire. I have already suggested a way in which we might read the
speech in terms of two distinct voices, two conflicting imperatives
addressed to a scarcely defined third figure, but it is easy to see how a
humanist criticism foregrounds this third figure, the 'real' Wendoll,
neither good nor evil but knowing in his uncertainty and so
imaginative, tormented.

Who is speaking when Hamlet castigates himself for his inaction?
A rogue and peasant slave? The 'I' of the utterance is here identified
as other, the 'I' of misrecognition, in contrast to the 'I' which
recognises the failure to act as inadequate, something to castigate.
That 'I', the distinct, differed subject of the enunciation, is the
humanist subject, the sensitive prince. And yet Hamlet's subjectivity
is itself un-speakable since the subject of the enunciation always
exceeds the subject of the utterance. Hamlet cannot be fully present
to himself or to the audience in his own speeches and *this* is the heart
of his mystery, his interiority, his essence.

One final instance: Macbeth contemplating the deep damnation
which is the inevitable consequence of Duncan's murder.

And pity, like a naked new-born babe,
Striding the blast, or heaven's cherubin hors'd
Upon the sightless couriers of the air,
Shall blow the horrid deed in every eye,
That tears shall drown the wind. I have no spur
To prick the sides of my intent, but only
Vaulting ambition, which o'er-leaps itself,
And falls on th' other.

                                        (I.vii.21–8)

An early seventeenth-century audience, well-versed in the emblematic tradition, might have attended primarily to two major figures: on the one hand, pity, 'like a naked new-born babe', and on the other a common medieval representation of pride, a knight who spurs his horse forward beyond its powers until he is thrown to the ground. For such an audience the imagery linking the elemental and the human ('tears shall drown the wind'), and the human and the supernatural (the babe and heaven's cherubin), might indicate that the hero's choice between pity and pride/ambition is a moment in the cosmic struggle with which he is continuous and which is duplicated in his own being. This is conjecture. Less conjecturally, a humanist criticism attends to two quite different figures, the subject of the utterance confronting a moral choice, and the subject who speaks, who identifies in cosmic imagery the perils of his own ambition. In the gap between them it constructs the feeling, self-conscious, 'poetic' Macbeth, a full subject, a character. The text, of course, internalising the emblems, reproducing them as verbal imagery, faces both ways. There is no single, correct 'historical' reading. But the reading we choose is produced by and produces in its turn a specific history which is always a history of the present. Liberal humanism finds its own reflection, its own imaginary fulness everywhere.

Whichever reading we choose there is a price to pay. To read these Renaissance soliloquies in their historical difference is to surrender liberal humanism's claims to universality and nature. Conversely, the subject of liberal humanism can never in practice control meaning, never mean exactly what is said, say exactly what is meant. Because the speaker necessarily exceeds the 'I' of the utterance, the unity promised by humanism inevitably eludes it. The humanist subject is always other than itself, can never be what it speaks. However much Hamlet tries to define the nature of true heroism, to analyse whether it is nobler to act or to suffer, a humanist knowledge finds that he is really thinking about suicide in the famous soliloquy. However he struggles to define revenge, to differentiate it from hire and salary, to identify it as an act which sends its victim to hell, humanist criticism finds him really rationalising his own continued delay. The sensitive prince does not mean what Hamlet says because the self is always ultimately un-speakable, unuttered.

And so the unified and unique subject of liberal humanism is forever tragically locked within its own silence, uncommunicating, granted the gift of language only in order inevitably to betray itself. In twentieth-century literature, where at last there is nothing that cannot be said, where the final barriers of censorship and self-censorship have fallen, there is in the end nothing worth saying because words finally fail to render the subject transparent to itself: for Prufrock, 'It is impossible to say just what I mean'; Beckett's doomed figures speak without signifying; Pinter's alienated characters bombard each other with empty clichés in a discourse which is always and evidently the discourse of the Other.

Humanist criticism is predicated on the subject's inability to express the meaning of which the subject is nonetheless the origin. Treating all texts as utterances, it undertakes to redouble them with another meaning, what the author really meant, what we as readers are meant to understand. The project is to remedy the author's inevitable failure. The quarry is the enunciating subject itself, source of the meaning only shadowed in the text. Literary criticism is thus a choric elegy for lost presence.

It is also, however, a way of controlling knowledge, of ruling out the plurality of readings the text as text is able to release, in favour of a single meaning which must always be uncovered by a certain expertise, a fineness of judgement not given to all readers, because the meaning in question is neither in the text nor produced by the text but is always elsewhere. Lost presence is reconstructed by a knowledge which comes from outside both the text and the consciousness of the enunciating subject.

True meaning is thus unconscious. And if humanist literary criticism offers to control our reading of texts, a humanist psychoanalysis is also there to control from outside the meaning of what we say, to identify what is really being said on that other scene beyond the censoring mechanisms of condensation and displacement. In psychoanalysis 'a thing must always mean something other than itself'; the truth of the utterance is to be found only 'by juggling with clues and significances'.[13] But there is *a* truth, a meaning, which arrests the play of signification. And this truth is always familial, always located in the patient's childhood, always in the past and not the present, with the effect of negating a present whose real meaning is somewhere else. What is more, the practice of psychoanalysis is directed inwards towards the absent self. In the process of transference the patient's emotions are relived and redirected to the silent analyst.

> The psychoanalytical transference, like a kind of churn for creaming off the reality of desire, leaves the patient dangling in a vertigo of

nothingness, a narcissistic passion which, though less dangerous than Russian roulette, leads if successful to the same sort of irreversible fixation on unimportant details which ends by withdrawing him from all other social investments.

(ibid.)

It all helps, of course, and this is Guattari's point, to keep us off the streets. The quest for the truth of the self, our own and others', endlessly fascinating, is precisely endless, since the subject of liberal humanism is a chimera, an effect of language, not its origin. Meanwhile, the social and political are placed as secondary concerns – naturally, since our democratic institutions are so clearly expressive of what we essentially are. In the subject's hopeless pursuit of self-presence politics can safely be left to take care of itself. And we can be sure that the institutions in question will in consequence stay much as they are.

From Catherine Belsey, *The Subject of Tragedy: Identity and Difference in Renaissance Drama* (London and New York, 1985), pp. 8–9, 33–5, 42–54.

NOTES

[Catherine Belsey has allowed us to take three extracts from her book *The Subject of Tragedy*, showing her poststructuralist argument about the development of subjectivity in early-modern England and including discussion of two soliloquies from *Macbeth*. Traditional criticism, Belsey holds, has looked for unified human subjectivities in literature, but Shakespeare and his contemporaries knew, in part at least, that the 'I' which speaks is always larger than the 'I' of the utterance. Shakespeare's plays are quoted from *The Complete Works*, ed. Peter Alexander (London, 1951). Ed.]

1. Daniel Rogers, *Matrimoniall Honour* (London, 1642), p. 189.

2. John Milton, *The Complete Prose Works*, vol. 2, ed. Ernest Sirluck (London, 1959), p. 242.

3. Richard Brathwait, *The English Gentleman; and the English Gentlewoman; Both in One Volume Couched* (London, 1641), pp. 32–4.

4. John Milton, *Poems*, ed. John Carey and Alastair Fowler (London, 1968), p. 477.

5. Raymond Williams, *Culture* (London, 1981), p. 142.

6. Antony Easthope, *Poetry as Discourse* (London, 1983), pp. 51–77, 94–109.

7. *Dr Faustus*, in Christopher Marlowe, *The Complete Works*, vol. 2, ed. Fredson Bowers (Cambridge, 1973), ll.1887–9.

8. *Everyman*, in Edgar T. Schell and J. D. Schuchter (eds), *English Morality Plays and Interludes* (New York, 1969), ll.85–183.

9. Thomas Kyd, *The Spanish Tragedy*, ed. Philip Edwards (London, 1959), III.xiii.1–44.

10. Thomas Heywood, *A Woman Killed with Kindness*, ed. R. W. van Fossen (London, 1961), III.422–52.

11. F. R. Leavis, *The Common Pursuit* (Harmondsworth, 1962), p. 152.

12. *The Castle of Perseverance*, in Mark Eccles (ed.), *The Macro Plays* (London, 1969), ll.281–2.

13. Felix Guattari, *Molecular Revolution*, trans. Rosemary Sheed (Harmondsworth, 1984), p. 55.

8

Speculations: 'Macbeth' and Source

JONATHAN GOLDBERG

'Shakespeare deals freely with his source', so Frank Kermode writes, considering the relationship of *Macbeth* to Holinshed. 'The actual words of Holinshed are closely followed, notably in IV.ii, but Shakespeare deals freely with his source, making Duncan old and venerable, instead of a young and weak-willed man. This is part of the general blackening of Macbeth's character'.[1] Geoffrey Bullough marvels at 'Shakespeare, with that wonderful memory ever ready to float up, albeit unconsciously, associations from reading or hearsay'. Thus, these critics affirm, Shakespeare moves freely in Holinshed, drawing on many narratives to fashion his 'composite picture', as Bullough calls it;[2] and whereas, in Holinshed, Duncan is both a good king and a weak one, and Macbeth is, at first loyal and then traitorous, Shakespeare – so the common line has it – recombines and simplifies his materials to offer a saintly king and his villainous murderer, and thereby makes differences clear-cut. Holinshed's narrative, because it motivates Macbeth's rebellion by allowing for defects in Duncan's rule (Duncan bars Macbeth's right to succeed to the throne, after all), takes an about-face when Macbeth turns tyrant; his earlier service to the king is labelled 'counterfet' (Bullough, p. 498). Shakespeare, according to Kermode, does not have Holinshed's problem; his Macbeth is 'blackened' from the start. The start? Where does a 'composite' text begin?

Such a question, I would argue, must be raised, and with it the common assumptions about Shakespeare, implicit in these descrip-

92

tions of the relationship of *Macbeth* to Holinshed, can begin to be investigated. For the assumption about the autonomous imagination of the author is allied to a description of a text remarkable for its moral clarity and its political conservatism – a description that may reveal more about the critics than about the play.

To test these commonplaces, let us take as an example Duncan's musing on the treacherous Thane of Cawdor:

> There's no art
> To find the mind's construction in the face:
> He was a gentleman on whom I built
> An absolute trust
>
> (I.iv.11–14)

These lines, cut short by the entrance of Macbeth, are generally seen as an index to the innocence of Duncan's mind. What is their source? In Holinshed, Duncan's words are spoken by a witch. She prophesies that the 'trustie servant' of King Natholocus, who has come to her on his ruler's behalf, will murder his monarch. The king, she says, will be killed by one 'in whome he had reposed an especiall trust' (Bullough, p. 478).

Duncan's lines, especially as they have been read most usually, suggest clear-cut moral differences. Yet that other habit of Shakespearean composition, its 'free' association, might lead one to ask if it is significant that Duncan voices lines spoken elsewhere by a witch. The question resonates if one allows another echo to sound, the reverberations of the witches' greeting of Macbeth – 'All hail Macbeth! hail to thee, Thane of Cawdor! / All hail, Macbeth! that shall be King hereafter' (I.iii.49–50) – reverberations that come to occupy Duncan's mouth. Just a few lines after the witches' allhailing, messengers from the king arrive, bid to 'call' Macbeth 'Thane of Cawdor: / In which addition, hail, most worthy Thane' (105–6); a scene later, Duncan names the king to be, 'Our eldest, Malcolm; whom we name hereafter' (I.iv.38). The text of *Macbeth* is itself 'composite', redistributing the witches' lines.

Is it to be accounted to the *free* dealing of the author's mind that Duncan's lines have their source – in Holinshed, in the play – in the mouths of witches? We might notice, too, that where Duncan swerves from the lines in Holinshed describing a king *reposing* his *special* trust, he substitutes the *activity* of *building* an *absolute* trust, and recall that Shakespeare drops Holinshed's description of Macbeth as master-builder of Dunsinane, virtually the only incident from

Macbeth's career not duplicated in the play, and allows Duncan instead to comment on the architecture of Inverness, thus permitting Duncan's to be the constructing mind. In short, the absolute differences and moral clarity that critics have found to be Shakespeare's are, at least in these instances, Duncan's. Monarch of the *absolute*, Duncan constructs differences against the demonic source of his lines, spoken by a witch and to a figure that serves as a model for Macbeth. Duncan's musings on the betrayal of the Thane of Cawdor have always been allowed the ironic echo that extends to the newly named Thane, Macbeth; the lines, I would suggest, might also be thought of as self-reflective. 'There's no art / To find the mind's construction in the face'; has not criticism − with scarcely an exception − succumbed to Duncan's glassy surface?

That surface is cut into again if we return to the source of Duncan's lines in Holinshed. For Holinshed also describes King Duff as one 'having a special trust in Donwald' (Bullough, p. 481), the loyal retainer that slays him. Holinshed's King Duff is a haunted and sleepless figure who sends his trusty servant to try to discover the cause of his disease. Donwald, the servant, finds a witch 'rosting upon a wooodden broch an image of wax at the fier, resembling in each feature the kings person' (p. 480). The king's illness is the result of this demonic voodoism, spectral identification, and he is restored to health as soon as Donwald destroys the waxen image. It scarcely needs mention that Holinshed's King Duff is − except for the line that Duncan speaks − a version of Macbeth. Does the spectre of identification drawn from the composition of Holinshed in *Macbeth* signify in the play? Both Duff and Donwald are versions of Macbeth. Duncan is a further spectral emanation of a source less intent on *absolute difference* than on resemblance. After King Duff is cured, he celebrates his recovery by making a 'spectacle' (Bullough, p. 481) of hanged rebels. Among them are Donwald's kin, and the loyal retainer who cured the king by destroying his spectre turns on the king who has made the spectacle. So, *Macbeth* opens with reports of Macbeth fixing a rebel head upon the battlements (I.ii.23) and closes with his severed head displayed by Macduff (V.ix.20); a plot inscribed and generated within specularity: in each instance, a supposedly saintly king has let another do his dirty work.

As another example of specular contamination, consider this episode from Holinshed: King Kenneth, successor to King Duff and murderer of his son and heir, suffers guilt and sleeplessness; he is told by prophetic voices that he will die and that the heir he has named will not succeed to the throne. His murder is accomplished by Fenella, avenging the death of her son, another child killed by the guilty monarch. Knowing 'that the king delighted above measure in goodlie buildings' (Bullough, p. 486), she constructs an elaborate tower covered with engraved flowers and other images. 'In the middest of the house there was a goodlie brasen image also, resembling the figure of king Kenneth' (Bullough, p. 487) holding in his hands a golden apple which, if plucked, activates crossbows aimed at the taker. The king succumbs to the lure and is killed. Whose career is this in *Macbeth*, Macbeth's . . . or Duncan's?

Macbeth looks in his conscience, torn by demonic representations and by Duncan's furthering of their designs; in soliloquy, he produces the saintly king – as a mirror. 'This Duncan / Hath borne his faculties so meek, hath been / So clear in his great office, that his virtues / Will plead like angels' (I.vii.16–19). Duncan's polished surface: is it the representation of an absolute power or the mirror of resemblance?

Duncan articulates, constructs, absolute difference, but equivocation arises from the source. 'People wished', Holinshed writes,

> the inclinations and maners of these two cousins to have beene so tempered and enterchangeablie bestowed betwixt them, that where the one had too much of clemencie, and the other of crueltie, the meane vertue betwixt these two extremities might have reigned by indifferent partition in them both.
>
> (Bullough, p. 488)

So, Lady Macbeth fears her husband 'is too full o' th' milk of human kindness' (I.v.17); so, as Harry Berger has persuasively argued, the opening scenes of the play enact an elaborately concealed hostility between Duncan and Macbeth, scenes, that is, of rivalry between characters who represent (in Holinshed's words) the 'indifferent partition' that 'reign[s]' in *Macbeth*.[3] 'Have we eaten on the insane root, / That takes the reason prisoner?' (I.iii.84–5), Banquo asks after the witches appear. The 'insane root' lies in the source; in Holinshed, Duncan disables the rebels by feeding them a poisoned brew that puts them to sleep. 'Look up clear', Lady Macbeth counsels her husband (I.v.71), and he looks in a mirror, to find Duncan, 'clear in his great office' (I.vii.18). Succession in the play can never take place except in a mirror. Macbeth invents the sainted king; he is not visible in the lines he speaks. After Macbeth kills him, he reports that Duncan's silver skin was breached with golden blood (II.iii.110). Such images are the obstacles that Macbeth finds in his path; they are also the source of his own legitimation when he comes to occupy Duncan's place. Macbeth succeeds as the king of the image repertoire in *Macbeth*.

Thus, when one looks to the most apparently straightforward scene of the transmission of source – the recasting of Holinshed's conversation between Macduff and Malcolm in IV.iii., what one discovers is that something has come between the source and the scene. What blocks the way of transmission is the text of *Macbeth* itself; Malcolm and Macduff repeatedly echo words and phrases that have come before, words most often heard in Macbeth's mouth. Resemblance, not difference, dominates the text; Macbeth attempts unpartnered to occupy alone what occupies him, to the end 'wrought / With things forgotten' (I.iii.151).

'People wished the inclinations and maners of these two cousins to have beene so tempered and enterchangeablie bestowed betwixt them', so Holinshed writes; is that desire, articulated in the source, also Shakespeare's? The chance and wayward associations of his 'wonderful memory'? The floating of his unconscious? A conscious design? To consider these questions, another source must be considered, the occasion of the play, for it is equally a critical commonplace to see the author of *Macbeth* succumbing to the exigencies of history, and to regard the play as a royal compliment: Edward the Confessor touches for the King's Evil as James, reluctantly, did; Banquo fathered James's line. Moreover, the text of *Macbeth* that we have derives from a court performance. Could Shakespeare have represented the contaminations of spectral resemblance before James I? Intentionally? Secretly? These questions about source lead to what Fredric Jameson might call the *political unconscious* of the play, a determined heterogeneity rather than the freeplay of the mind.[4] What, we need to ask, are the political conditions of representation in which *Macbeth* is located?

The text of *Macbeth* offers one index to these conditions, for it is, as Stephen Orgel has remarked,[5] a palimpsest, combining at least two versions of the play; one version dates from the time of the Gunpowder Plot, and is alluded to, for instance, by the Porter's use of *equivocation* in the play (II.iii.; and also, at V.v.43, by Macbeth); another version is several years later, and is marked by the additions of songs from Middleton's *The Witch*, a play presumed to postdate Jonson's 1609 *Masque of Queens*. From Act III on, if not before, the text of *Macbeth* shows signs of tampering: transposed scenes, cut lines, wholesale interpolations of songs and dances. The menacing powers of the witches are trivialised, and to reduce the impact of their show of kings they propose to 'cheer . . . up' Macbeth:

> Come, sisters, cheer we up his sprites,
> And show the best of our delights.
> I'll charm the air to give a sound,
> While you perform your antic round;
> That this great King may kindly say,
> Our duties did his welcome pay.
>   (IV.i.127–32)

Who is 'this great King' to whom compliment is paid, if not the monarch in the audience? The text alludes to the presence of King James in this compliment as well as in the formal accommodations that make the text of *Macbeth* masquelike. But even these trivial lines of jaunty welcome to the king enact a curious play of resemblance. The editor of the Arden edition of *Macbeth*, for example, takes 'this great King' to refer to Macbeth. One king slides into the other, a type of diffusion that can be remarked elsewhere in the latter half of *Macbeth*, in the withdrawal of Lady Macbeth and her replacement with Lady Macduff, or in the English scenes with their echoes of Scottish horror; we see less of Macbeth as the play proceeds, and hear more of him. The presence of King James in the text of *Macbeth*, however much it disturbs the original and irrecoverable designs of the play, also seems to be written within them. Might we say that the earlier relationship between Macbeth and Duncan is re-enacted between Macbeth and King James? That there is room in the text for only one king? That these two monarchs are haunted by spectral identification? A mirror, literally, provides an answer to these speculations. In the show of kings, Macbeth looks into the mirror in which James I is reflected:

> . . . the eighth appears, who bears a glass
> Which shows me many more; and some I see,
> That two-fold balls and treble sceptres carry.
> Horrible sight!
>   (IV.i.119–22)

Disturbing the notion of clear-cut difference in this confrontation is, once again, the problem of source, for the show of kings is provided by the 'filthy hags' (l.115), and however much their subsequent jauntiness seems to diffuse the spectacle, it retains its disturbing power. Steven Mullaney has written wonderfully about this moment, about the alliance of the demonic to a linguistic excess. As he says, in that mirroring moment

> genealogy and prophecy are made manifest in a visible display, but there is another genealogy in the air as well, one heard rather than seen. Juxtaposed to the projection of James's line, the witches' riddles complicate its complimentary gesture with what amounts to a genealogy of treason and equivocation.[6]

If earlier Duncan spoke witches' words, here the king is transported on stage in the witches' show, caught within speculation. If earlier Duncan bestowed gifts and titles to 'name' a 'hereafter' already named, here James is asked to 'kindly say' that the witches' 'duties did his welcome pay'. The king lives to bestow, as James indicated when he titled his treatise on kingship the *Basilikon Doron*, the royal gift. His gift was his presence and the heir he produced; presentation that is re-presentation. There is an economy of speculation.

Is the show of kings subversive? Do its spectral identifications implicate Shakespeare in a revolutionary politics? Could such a politics evade the reflections of a mirror that catches the king on stage and off? Is there an autonomous realm available for representation that would not be caught within representation? That realm of autonomy, Franco Moretti suggests, is coincident with sovereignty imagined as 'a power ... having its origin *in itself*'.[7] When James represented that power, as in the sonnet prefatory to the *Basilikon Doron*, he declared himself a god by announcing that 'God gives not Kings the stile of *Gods* in vaine'; the king who gives all has been given his power as a *style*, and as an echoing name. The king stands *in the place* of the 'heavenly King', his 'Lieutenant'. Duncan dresses Macbeth in borrowed robes as well, making a voodoo version of himself. 'Remember', James counselled his son and heir, 'the throne is Gods and not yours, that ye sit in'.[8] Presenting himself, claiming all his kingdom as his own – the kingdom was his body and his wife, he declared on more than one occasion – James also saw himself as representation, a king on stage, whose behaviour offered a living 'image' of himself. Royal existence is representation. 'Let your owne life be a law-booke and a mirrour to your people' (p. 30), James urged his son in the book in which he similarly presented himself, counselling him to present himself as the 'vive image' of his 'vertuous disposition' (p. 51). Offering himself to parliamentary inspection, the king was fond of declaring that his breast was a crystal mirror, both a reflecting surface and a transparent one. What could one's 'owne life' be in such formulations of identity – even absolute identity – as reflection? Wouldn't this hall of mirrors include the notion of 'a power . . . having its origin *in itself*' – whether we were to attach that idea of autonomy to the king or to the sovereign author of *Macbeth*? Could there be an end to these speculations, or a source?

Ben Jonson's masques for King James frequently depend upon such absolutist assertions and they are our best guide to the conditions of absolutist representation in the Jacobean period. When Jonson wrote a masque celebrating James's birthday in 1620, the king was cast as Pan, for Pan means 'all': 'Pan is our all, by him we breathe, we live, / We move, we are'.[9] Yet, included in the spectacle that Jonson offered the king were disturbing reflections of himself and his courtiers, particularly in the figure of a court ape outrageously parodying the court. Jonson showed James how to view the attack by reprimanding the parodist in the masque. 'Your folly may well deserve pardon because it hath delighted', he is told; 'but beware of presuming, or how you offer comparisons with persons so near deities. Behold where they are that have now forgiven you, whom should you provoke again with the like, they will justly punish that with anger which they now dismiss with contempt' (ll.131–6). The court and its parodist face each other in this moment to regard one another within the spectacle of 'comparisons' and resemblances; the derisory spectacle is to be seen with derision. James must forgive all if all reflects him and if he is the ultimate source of all representation. In Jonson's masques, the representation of the king's claims to totality offers the possibility of endless replications within the system of reflecting power in which the king was placed. ...

Jonson's *Masque of Queens* is particularly apt for consideration here because, like *Macbeth*, central to its concerns is a contention between royal and demonic powers and, specifically, the question of the source of power. [The masque] is palpably dualistic in design. It opens with 'a foil or false masque' (l.12) in which eleven witches invoke their Dame. She arrives and the witches join together as 'faithful opposites' (l.120) to 'disturb' the entertainment – and, more frighteningly, to oppose the accomplishments of an 'Age of Gold' (l.129) and return all things to chaos. The Dame proposes their plans in these words:

> Let us disturb it then, and blast the light;
> Mix hell with heaven, and make Nature fight

Within herself; loose the whole hinge of things,
And cause the ends run back into their springs.
(ll.134–7)

Gathering together the elements necessary for their powers, the Dame attempts to raise a spirit to accomplish their task. She fails, and in the midst of their frenzied dances, loud music and a sudden change of scene usher in Perseus, the figure of Heroic Virtue, announcing the arrival of Fame; she, in turn, brings on a consort of twelve heroic queens, who end the masque in dancing. Virtue has triumphed over vice; as Jonson notes at the climactic change of scene, the hags vanish 'scarce suffering the memory of such a thing' (l.337).

'Scarce suffering' – barely permitting, but yet, not entirely effacing. For, as is apparent even in a brief summary of the action of the masque, the forces of good and evil bear a striking resemblance – 12 hags, 12 queens – and the structure of the two halves of the masque is also broadly parallel – invocations, arrivals, dances. Dualism would seem to be a mirror effect. In *Queens*, moreover, language passes through the mirror, overriding differences. Although ostensibly the two parts of the masque are related only by opposition, and although the second half of the masque removes all traces of the first, the language of the masque is seamless. Its central trope, in fact, involves sources and origins, suggesting an overriding power. Jonson announces that the argument of the masque is 'true fame bred out of virtue' (l.6); yet breeding, arrival, origination are everywhere apparent in the masque, throwing the relationship between the two parts into question. Does the second come from the first? Has the Dame's unsuccessful attempt to raise a spirit issued in the arrival of Heroic Virtue? Is there a beginning principle?

Here in any event is the seamless thread: the witches arrive, claiming they 'come . . . from' a landscape replete with death (ll.45–54), and as they try repeated charms, naming all their instruments (owls, baying dogs, toads, voodoo images, and the like), they raise their Dame. More invocations follow, filled with snatchings, gatherings, pluckings, choosing, biting, sucking, getting, and making – a depletion and a dismemberment of nature to reconstitute it in the spectre they would raise. The earth is made a grave, they bury (l.230) what they have gathered and seek to make it rise again, reconstituted. Here, the language of birth that underlies all these activities is made explicit:

> Dame earth shall quake,
> And the houses shake,
> And her belly shall ache
> As her back were brake
> Such a birth to make
> (ll.240–4)

At first they are unsuccessful – 'our labor dies! / Our magic feature will not rise' (ll.269–70) – and they attempt again their 'magic birth' (l.298). Instead, the House of Fame rises 'in the place of' (l.338) the witches' hell, as the stage direction indicates. Perseus declares himself the 'parent' (l.356) of Fame; Fame arrives acknowledging her 'father' (l.431) and announcing that she will 'draw ... forth' (l.439) the twelve queens, who sing in celebration of 'Fame that's out of Virtue born' (l.487) and 'this famous birth' (l.500).

These continuities would seem to confirm the Dame's design, mixing hell with heaven, loosing the 'whole hinge of things', and making endings fetch their origins in chaotic beginnings – the scarce-remembered, almost vanished traces of a design which the masque replicates even as it replaces it. If we ask why this spectre of resemblance should be in the masque, the answer, we may assume, has to do with absolutist power. Power in the masque is figured as origin giving. Perseus is both parent and strength (l.356); like the witches, he makes life from death: 'When Virtue cut off Terror, he gat [i.e. begat] Fame. / ... when Fame was gotten Terror died' (ll.351–2). As much as the witches, he needs to dismember to make. Powers of making depend upon depletion – and this, too, is how the masque itself is constructed, 'scarce suffering' the memory of the displaced hags, but not entirely effacing them. Jonson's making is thus also in question. Although Perseus points to the columns of the House of Fame as 'men-making poets' (l.362), the poet of the masque is at pains to disavow his powers, telling his reader (Prince Henry) that the masque's invention comes from the queen (ll.9–10); that the decorum of the masque derives from Horace (ll.7–8); that the queens and witches are drawn from the storehouse of classical and contemporary books that he has perused; that even the spectators give life to his designs: 'a writer should always trust somewhat to the capacity of the spectator, especially at these spectacles' (ll.95–6).

The privileged spectator here is the king, of course, and the spectacle is designed to mirror and bring forth his mind. Hence, when Perseus presents the twelve queens, he ends with the king, and although Bel-Anna (Queen Anne's role in the masque) is the highest of queens, she must submit 'all her worth / To him that gave it', the one who has 'brought forth / Their names to memory' (ll.402–4). The pronoun may refer to the poet; a few lines later, it means the king, source of all 'increase' (l.410), conferring the bounty on all which is 'contracted' (l.412) within himself. The king, Perseus says, will 'embrace' the 'spectacle' (ll.414–15). From a 'spectacle of strangeness, producing multiplicity of gesture' (ll.17–18), as Jonson describes the antimasque of witches, arises 'the strangeness and beauty of the spectacle' (l.466), the genuine masque of queens. What the text produces is referred to the king's eye.

What lives in the king's eye here, as in *Macbeth*, is genealogy, what he produces; here, as in *Macbeth*, the king lives to bestow, to give gifts which are contracted within him and which are extended without. Royal absolutism is coincident with full ownership and extension over all so that nothing and no one has autonomy except the king; yet this means that, like Duncan, his absolutism also signifies opacity. The king who gives all is appropriated by what he appropriates. Building and constructing all in his all-embracing view, his power is his blindness. His power lies in a mirror whose reflections cannot be controlled: speculative investments that may deplete the all-giver. Duncan and Macbeth meet for the first time in the play, and Duncan voices the depletion involved in giving, the horrific sense that their exchanges are spectral identifications, transfers like the voodoo magic between the king and his replica:

> O worthiest cousin!
> The sin of my ingratitude even now
> Was heavy on me. Thou art so far before,
> That swiftest wing of recompense is slow
> To overtake thee: would thou hadst less deserv'd,
> That the proportion both of thanks and payment
> Might have been mine! Only I have left to say,
> More is thy due than more than all can pay.
>   (I.iv.14–21)

The more he gives, the less he has; his wish: 'would thou hadst less deserv'd.' A few lines later, Duncan attempts to name the 'hereafter' despite Macbeth's success, 'so far before'.

*

On August 27, 1605, in the course of a visit James and his family made to Oxford, they were welcomed to St John's College by a learned show, a Latin entertainment hailing the fulfilment of fate's prophesied genealogy (the line of Banquo) embodied in the king and queen and their heirs. The lines were spoken by three woodland creatures, 'quasi Sibyllae', they are called, boys masquerading as numinous female powers, all-hailing their monarch (Bullough, p. 471):

> Fame says the fatal Sisters once foretold
> Power without end, great Monarch, to thy stock . . .
> And thus we greet thee: Hail, whom Scotland serves!
> Whom England, Hail! Whom Ireland serves, all hail!

So, too, the witches greet Macbeth, so Duncan gives addition to the new Thane of Cawdor. Banquo wonders if the witches can speak true, but the echoes go back further. The witches' all-hailing inaugurates Macbeth's career by appropriating a moment of royal compliment. From the start, the mirror of representation respects no boundaries; the show of kings staged for the mutual benefit of Macbeth and King James occurs *within* these representations. There is no source, not even a sovereign author, outside of representation, no end or beginning to these speculations.

✢

Within *Macbeth*, the menacing heterogeneity of uncontrolled duplication that threatens the autonomy of power is embodied in the witches. In the anxiety about women in the play we might find a further reflection of the disturbing questions raised about the sources of the Shakespearean imagination. Jonson's *Masque of Queens* is instructive in that regard as well, for in order to represent sovereign power, woman's control over nature and birth are ascribed to the king. Perseus declares his power – to give birth – and refers it to the king's bounty. Yet, what is presented to the monarch's eyes is a pageant of armed women to replace the army of hags, a haunting version of the king's declaration of patriarchal appropriations. Questions about a power that 'lies like truth' (*Macbeth*, V.v.44) menace men's words and their assertions of authority. Kings and authors, then, are menaced. . . .

The hypermasculine world of *Macbeth* is haunted – as is *The*

Masque of Queens – by the power represented in the witches; masculinity in the play is directed as an assaultive attempt to secure power, to maintain success and succession, at the expense of women. As is typical of many of Shakespeare's tragedies, the play is largely womanless and family relationships are disturbed; Duncan and Banquo both have heirs, but no wives; Macbeth and Lady Macbeth have no surviving children. The one fully gratuitous act of Macbeth's is the murder of Lady Macduff and her children, an act in which Macduff is fully complicit; he has abandoned his wife, and she accuses him of betrayal. He allies himself with Malcolm in a scene in which the future monarch displays his credentials first by presenting himself as excessively libidinous – and Macduff willingly responds as a virtual procurer to satisfy his lust – and then as excessively chaste; either way, masculinity and power are directed against women. When Macbeth is finally defeated, he is replaced by two men who have secured power in the defeat of women. Indeed, Macduff has not only abandoned his wife and family, his very birth represents a triumph over his mother's womb, the manifest fantasy of being self-begotten that also deludes Macbeth in his final encounter. To mark the new powers in Scotland, the battle concludes with Siward's celebration of the ritual slaughter of his son. It is not Macbeth alone who opposes generativity or wishes to eradicate its source. Good and bad Scots alike are bent on securing power, and that means to seize fully the terrain of women. For Scotland is a bleeding mother in the play, and their aim is to 'bestride our downfall birthdom' (IV.iii.4). 'It cannot / Be call'd our mother, but our grave' (ll.165–6), Rosse goes on to say. Birth and death are, in these paradigmatic utterances, man's downfall, the limits of beginning and end; they survive his successes, unlimited limits. The seizure and defeat of women is a bid for immortality, for a power that will never fade.

The shape of that fantasy is revealed in the mirror scene; a line of kings propagated in the mirror. Males produce males, just as Banquo and Duncan seem capable of succession without the interference of women. 'Look in thy glass, and tell the face thou viewest / Now is the time that face should form another'; so the third sonnet opens on the prospect of a duplication of images that might be called – if we follow Luce Irigaray – a determining patriarchal fantasy, the glassy façade of 'the sovereign authority of pretense'.[10] Macbeth looks in the mirror and sees his reflection in the line that extends to James; not in the mirror is Mary Queen of Scots, the figure that haunts the patriarchal claims of the *Basilikon Doron*, the mother on whom

James rested his claims to the throne of England – and whom he sacrificed to assure his sovereignty.

Men may look in the mirror, may have their being in the mirror; but in *Macbeth*, the spectre of duplicates is in other hands. The spectacle of state here, or in *The Masque of Queens*, is the witches' show. All masculine attempts at female deprivation – including Lady Macbeth's desire to unsex herself – are robbed of ultimate success. Mortality cannot be killed. What escapes control is figured in the witches; emblematically bearded, linguistically ambiguous, they represent, in Harry Berger's brilliant phrase, the textual 'display of withheld surplus meaning'.[11] Their words stretch out 'to th' crack of doom' (IV.i.117), an ultimate fissure in which both Macbeth and Malcolm have their place hereafter. ...

To think of history as heterogeneous dispersal is a political act. It calls into question those modes of 'logocentric, metaphysical, idealistic ... representation'[12] that ascribe determinate force to hegemonic rhetoric and that assume that ideological inscriptions really have the power they claim. It has instead been the argument of this paper that ideology is haunted by what it excludes, subverted by what it subordinates. Such an argument does not assume the possibility of some other mode of discourse (an Althusserian dream of science, for instance, 'outside' of ideology), for to do so would be to replace one form of idealism with another. And thus, in this paper, the terms which must be used – referring us to texts and authors and events – can only be taken as tropes, speculations with counters that discourse fills, but which cannot be contained; halls of mirrors in which resemblance does not halt. In that respect, this paper might be called 'The Mirror of Kings'. Although the argument I make seems to me congruent with the thesis of *James I and the Politics of Literature* (1983), there is a shift of emphasis in this paper. In that book I was interested in mapping strategies of representation shared by Jacobean authors and their monarch. This paper looks at the dark side of representation. The emphasis now is on the *re* in representation, the haunting spectre of duplication that unmoors texts and events from a positivistic view of history or literature. What is *real*, then, is the *re*, perhaps itself a recovery of the nothing into which things slide. Latin *rem* lies behind French *rien*.

From *Shakespeare Reproduced*, ed. Jean E. Howard and Marion F. O'Connor (New York and London, 1987), pp. 247–53, 254–7, 259–60, 247.

NOTES

[Jonathan Goldberg shares with other authors in this collection a broadly new historicist and poststructuralist concern with the instabilities that inevitably attend textuality and reading. Here, in an important extension and partial revision of Goldberg's argument in his *James I and the Politics of Literature* (Baltimore, 1983), these instabilities are traced not just to the subjectivities of writers and readers but to the historical situation of the play and of Shakespeare as writer. Professor Goldberg has agreed to shorten his essay and limit the scope of the notes. *Macbeth* is quoted from the New Arden edition, ed. Kenneth Muir (London, 1972). Ed.]

1. Frank Kermode, 'Introduction' to *Macbeth*, in *The Riverside Shakespeare* (Boston, 1974), p. 1308.

2. Geoffrey Bullough, *Narrative and Dramatic Sources of Shakespeare*, vol. 7 (London, 1973), pp. 444, 448; cited hereafter in the text as 'Bullough'.

3. Harry Berger, Jr., 'The Early Scenes of *Macbeth*: preface to a new interpretation', *English Literary History*, 47 (1980), pp. 1–31.

4. See Fredric Jameson, *The Political Unconscious: narrative as a socially symbolic act* (Ithaca and London, 1981).

5. Stephen Orgel, 'Shakespeare Imagines a Theater', in *Shakespeare, Man of the Theater*, ed. Kenneth Muir, Jay L. Halio and D. J. Palmer (Newark, 1983), p. 43.

6. Steven Mullaney, 'Lying like Truth: riddle, representation and treason in Renaissance England', *English Literary History*, 47 (1980), 41; reprinted in Mullaney's book, *The Place of the Stage* (Chicago, 1988). [A shortened version of this essay is reprinted in this volume – see p. 115. Ed.]

7. Franco Moretti, *Signs Taken For Wonders*, trans. David Miller (London, 1983), p. 45.

8. *Basilikon Doron*, in *The Political Works of James I*, ed. Charles H. McIlwain (Cambridge, Mass., 1918), p. 39.

9. Ben Jonson, *The Complete Masques*, ed. Stephen Orgel (New Haven, 1969), ll.170–1. In the following pages Jonson's masques are quoted from this edition.

10. Luce Irigaray, 'Des marchandises entre elles'; trans. Claudia Reeder in *New French Feminisms*, ed. Elaine Marks and Isabelle de Courtivron (Brighton, 1981), p. 189.

11. Harry Berger, 'Text Against Performance in Shakespeare: the example of *Macbeth*', *Genre*, 15 (1982), 52.

12. Jacques Derrida, *Positions*, trans. Alan Bass (Chicago, 1981), pp. 49–50.

9

Lying like Truth: Riddle, Representation, and Treason in Renaissance England

STEVEN MULLANEY

I

In 1600, violating ancient codes of hospitality and of fealty, the Earl of Gowrie attempted to murder James VI of Scotland while the sovereign was staying at Gowrie's house in Perth. Gowrie and his accomplice were cut down in the attempt. But according to *Gowries Conspiracie*, printed in the same year *cum privilegio Regis*, the Earl's corpse bore its wounds strangely. It refused to bleed until James, while searching the body for letters that might provide a clue to a deed inexplicable as that of a man acting under his own power and volition, discovered a 'close parchment bag' in Gowrie's pocket and removed it. Immediately blood gushed from the corpse. Nature resumed its course, and with nature and James once more in control, the body of the traitor was once again free, and once again subject to natural and human laws. It was free, that is, to be transported to Edinburgh, presented to Parliament in a spectral session, duly found guilty of treason, and then hanged, drawn and quartered, and exhibited – on poles fixed at Edinburgh, Perth, Dundee, and Stirling. Gowrie's bag was found to be 'full of magicall characters, and words of inchantment, wherein, it seemed, he put his confidence'.[1]

Today we are uncertain which to be most incredulous about – the documented spectacle of execution, or the preternatural detail of this 'devil's writ', as York describes the 'oracles ... hardly attained and hardly understood' that he snatches from Southwell's hand in *2 Henry VI* (I.iv.69). Both are significant aspects of the representation of treason in the age, however. The traitor stands at an uncertain threshold of Renaissance society, athwart a line that sets off the human from the demonic, the natural from the unnatural, and the rational from the enigmatic and obscure realm of unreason. Treason is a twice-monstrous act: it is something awesome and terrifying in a way we find difficult to conceive – although period accounts, such as those describing the mood of London after the discovery of the Gunpowder Plot in 1605,[2] testify to its tumultuous repercussions even in failure – but it is monstrous, too, in that it is something made to show and reveal itself in both speech and spectacle. The fate of the Gunpowder conspirators provides but one example of a sequence that was typical, and could be described as the penal variety of a 'King's Triumphs': first the confessions, then a procession through the city and an exhibition so that the populace could come to see the traitors 'as the rarest sorts of monsters; fools to laugh at them, women and children to wonder, and all the common people to gaze'.[3] In treason's procession as in the King's the city itself is the stage, and its streets form the scene for a mobile representation of power and authority. In the royal procession, however, the King himself appears and passes through a series of elaborate archways that provide, with their emblems and devices, a running commentary on his presence and his power. In chains as a sign and demonstration of that power, the traitor is himself a living gloss upon it and needs no further interpretation. But if his course is not graced in advance with the handiwork of the city's guilds, his wake is afterwards hung with treason's emblems. The final stage and ultimate performance of treason, often accompanied by a second, public confession, was of course on the scaffold, where the traitor was hanged and drawn and quartered for further display in death, according to a custom whose ritual was as much dramatic as it was juridical.

There are suggestive analogies to be drawn between the one scaffold and the other – between the spectacle of the traitor on the platform of public execution and on the stage – but it would be wrong to equate the two. It is not that one is real, however, while the other is a mere show. Each belongs to the ritual and representation of treason in the Renaissance, but with a crucial difference. It is not treason that speaks from the place of execution, and in a sense it is no longer the body of the traitor that is painstakingly subjected to the law, and so shown to be human and natural once again. Confession and execution mark the return of the traitor to society and to himself, even in death. 'Nothing in his life', as Malcolm says of the repentant Cawdor's execution, 'Became him like the leaving of it' (I.iv.7). His death was fitting and becoming, in a sense, because it was only in leaving life that he again became *himself* and achieved again a certain decorum of self – as Gowrie did even in death when his bag of riddles was removed. Confession, execution, and dismemberment, unsettling as they may seem, were not so much punishment of the traitor as they were the demonstration that what had been a traitor was no longer, and that what had set him off from man and nature had been, like Gowrie's bag, lifted from him. When the body bleeds, treason has been effaced; execution is treason's epilogue, spoken by the law. In histories of the period, however, treason presents us with a more equivocal figure; on stage, it is something closer to treason itself that is enacted, and that speaks.

II

It is during the country troubles of Henry VIII that the language of treason begins, like masterless men, to come under renewed legislative scrutiny. ... With the Treason Act of 1534, the explicit questioning of the King's authority becomes a matter of high treason, punishable by death. Making speech a capital offence provoked a long-lasting dispute with Parliament. ... But whenever troubles arise, what you say again becomes an affair of life and death. ...

But the rebel is rarely so accommodatingly forthright. He 'troubleth by biwaies', as Sir John Cheeke writes in *The Hurt of Sedicion* (1569): he wins others over to his cause not by outright, identifiable and therefore governable lies, but by relying upon and taking advantage of the multiple senses of things, whether actions or words. The rebel or traitor is not a plain dealer, quite the opposite. 'He cannot plainely withstand and useth subtilities of sophistrie', Cheeke continues, 'mistaking the thing, but persuading men's minds, and abusing the plaine meaning of the honest to a wicked end of religious overthrow'.[4] Cheeke confronts not treason's lie – so much is assumed – but the problem of its persuasiveness and the difficulty of identifying it in the making, before the damage is done and the rabble roused. Treason lies, but it lies like truth – as it must do. ...

Yet if the traitor abuses words, he is also abused by them. Among the causes of the Yorkshire uprising of 1549, amid a discussion of the rebels' grievances and evil dispositions, Holinshed notes that 'an other cause was, for trusting to a blind and fantasticall prophecie, where with they were seduced, thinking the same prophecie shuld come to passe, by the rebellions of Norffolke, of Devonshire, and other places'.[5] The Yorkshire rebels were as much the victims of this 'fantasticall prophecie' as they were its agents, and they were undone by the riddle that led them on with the hope of success. Here we encounter a recurrent topos in accounts of treason. ... In these prophecies and riddles what we might dismiss as mere superstition constitutes in fact a rhetoric of rebellion. 'When we speak or write doubtfully, that the sence may be taken in two ways', we are guilty, according to George Puttenham, of ambiguitas – or in the Greek, of amphibology. Puttenham ranks amphibology as the worst abuse or vice in rhetoric. ... If the traitor is an ambiguous figure for Holinshed, the vice or trope of amphibology is for Puttenham the figure of treason itself. ...[6]

Nor are they simply relics of bygone days, for amphibologies return wilfully to trouble both the still developing national language and the security of the state itself. ... According to period accounts the rebellion led by Robert Kett in 1549 was guided from beginning to end by 'fayned prophecies' that seemed to promise success to the rebels' cause but were in fact 'as ambiguous as those uttered by older and more famous soothsayers'. Obscure or doubtful as the riddles were, they possessed a persuasive force. 'Still there was a charm, and mystery, a mighty power to them'.[7] Kett's rebellion was a massive one. Following a minor enclosure riot at Attleborough in June of 1549, villagers gathered at Wymondham on July 7 to celebrate an annual festival and attend a play in honour of Thomas of Canterbury. More fences were torn down by the gathered crowd. A landlord himself, Kett joined the mob after his own fences were lost, organised it and led it as an army eventually numbering 16,000 men in a successful siege on Norwich. Locally impressed and royal troops were defeated, a royal pardon offered and rejected. When Kett found himself under attack by 11,000 troops under the Earl of Warwick it was an amphibological riddle that determined the course of what was intended to be a strategic retreat:

> The country gnoffes, Hob, Dick, and Hick
>> With clubbes and clouted shoone
>>> Shall fill the vale
>>>> Of Dussindale
> With slaughter'd bodies soon.[8]

Fill the vale they did: the oracle was fulfilled, although the bodies in the vale proved not to be, as the rebels had presumed they would, those of Warwick's men.

The riddle of treason lies, it seems, in the riddle itself. A riddle, a prophecy, a double meaning, an unsettling pun: 'when a sentence may be turned both wayes', Abraham Fraunce says of amphibole, 'so that a man shall be uncertayne what way to take.'[9] . . . A lie can be defined or outlawed, a veiled message unveiled. But these riddles, prophecies, or amphibologies involve something other than treason lying or disguising itself. They exceed and usurp the intentions of the traitor himself, bifurcating choice and intentionality. Surprisingly, no source is suggested for the prophecy in cases such as Kett's, no agent demonic or otherwise is even obliquely mentioned. The traitor is seduced by a language without origin.

But if amphibology seduces the traitor, it also presents authority with a considerable dilemma, and with it we move into a linguistic sphere the law cannot control, . . . beyond which authority can only watch and listen to treason's amphibolic spectacle.

III

In December of 1604 the Gowrie plot was briefly exhumed as *Gowrie*, a lost play performed at least twice by the King's Players and then banned with a minor rebuke to the company for having thus brought the King to the scaffold. While the direct representation of the King on stage might risk displeasure or imprisonment, the staging of treason – preternatural and regicidal as it might be – did not, and we can assume that Gowrie's 'magicall characters, and words of inchantment' made their appearance in the play. Some two years after presumably performing in *Gowrie*, a year after the Gunpowder Plot of 1605, one of the King's Players turned to Holinshed for the plot of a play rich in such elements, in which a Scottish King is assaulted by a kinsman and a subject – while in 'double trust,' as James was in 1600. *Macbeth* is perhaps the fullest literary representation of treason's amphibology in its age. In 1606 it was performed for James at court: authority watched, and listened. Onstage is a Scotland rapidly succumbing to misrule, lamented and viewed from an English perspective by its former countrymen – a description that fits the perspective of Malcolm and his fellow refugees from Macbeth's bloody reign, but one that fits the perspective of James as well, as he viewed the play. The Scotland on the scaffold is one preliminary to the intersection of James' line with Scottish royalty, but prophetic of it; it is also a Scotland interfused with contemporary concerns of the English court. But the fusion of times and places is not without its unsettling prospects from the vantage point of the throne.

Nearing the end of his fantastic career, Macbeth pauses and looks back down the way he has come, recognising behind him the doubtful crossroads and the way not taken in the riddles that once made him resolute, bloody and bold:

> I pull in resolution; and begin
> To doubt th'equivocation of the fiend,
> That lies like truth.
>
> (V.v.41)

He has recognised the amphibology in the witches' riddles – the duplicitous sense of 'wood' in the one prophecy wherein he put his confidence – and he will soon come to know that 'none of woman born' was not the impossible and inhuman reference he took it for, but rather paltered with him in a double sense of 'born'. In Macbeth's recognition the audience finds a peculiar one of its own. For recognising amphibology where one expected something more univocal has been the experience of the audience since Macbeth's drunken Porter made his entrance, so upsetting to Coleridge, and gave us his topical pronouncement. 'Faith, here's an equivocator, that could swear in both scales against either scale; who committed treason enough for Gods sake, yet could not equivocate to heaven' (II.iii.9).

In 1606 the topical reference was a clear one, since Father Garnet's equivocation during his trial for complicity in the Gunpowder Plot was still an active and much publicised concern. While the reference was clear, however, the *relation* of Garnet's equivocation to the play was not. In its narrow historical context, 'equivocation' has been of inestimable aid in dating *Macbeth*, but of doubtful use as a key to the entanglements of truth, lie, and treason in the play.[10] What Shakespeare gives us is not treason's lie – something that the court might well have expected, something it could regulate, define, control, and perhaps anticipate – but treason's amphibology. Not Garnet's equivocation, but an equivocation that lies like truth.

According to James, Garnet lied. According to the Church he relied upon a theologically valid duplicity known as equivocation or mental reservation – qualifying his spoken utterances with unspoken emendations, forming a true if mixed response to the questions put him. In the eyes (or ears) of God, he had not lied. During the sixteenth century the Church promulgated and defended such equivocation as a strategy for Catholics to employ when caught between conflicting demands for loyalty to Protestant rulers and to Rome, and it is equivocation as such – as mental reservation – that the audience of *Macbeth* had well in mind. The theological treatises on equivocation that begin with St Raymond's *Summa* (1235) describe mental reservation, however, as a secondary, narrower form of equivocation.[11] The term used for its primary form is amphibology. The Church had better sense, however, than to recommend punning under oath as a pragmatic strategy for Catholics who had to skate between the truth and a lie. Although theologically sound, puns and amphibologies would be of dubious value if *control* of a situation was paramount. As our tales of treason suggest, amphibology resists control. Indeed, psychoanalytic theory draws an antithetical relationship between control and amphibology, since it is through parapraxes and puns that the unconscious breaches the defences of the conscious mind.

When Thomas James refers to Garnet in 1612, he echoes Fraunce's syntax and image of amphibole as a crossroads where choice is bifurcated, but it is an empty echo. 'Al his Equivocations, wherein his tongue runs one way, and his meaning another, that you know not where to find him'.[12] The intentions of the speaker *rule* here: mental reservation resides and resolves itself in the conscious intentions of the speaker. In *Macbeth*, from its foul-and-fair opening to the senseless slaughter of Macduff's family in an effort to crown, as Macbeth says, his 'thoughts with acts', intention, act, and language are unruly, a matter of words unencompassed by definitions of truth and lie that 'palter with us in a double sense' and that exceed Macbeth's intentions and his efforts to control, both compelling and undoing his resolution.

Shakespeare does not, then, merely project the concerns of the moment onto the screen of Scotland's past. When finally admitted by the Porter, Macduff questions him, and the doorkeeper responds in 'multitudinous antitheses', glossing his previous reference to mental reservation with a demonstration of amphibology in comic guise, culminating in an (un)resolving pun on 'lie':

> **Macduff** What three things does drink especially provoke?
>
> **Porter** Marry, sir, nose-painting, sleep, and urine. Lechery, sir, it provokes and unprovokes: it provokes the desire, but it takes away the performance. Therefore, much drink may be said an equivocator with lechery: it makes him, and it mars him; it sets him on, and it takes him off; it persuades him, and it disheartens him; makes him stand to, and not stand to: in conclusion, equivocates him in a sleep, and, giving him the lie, leaves him.
>
> (II.iii.26)

It is when Macbeth returns to the heath and seeks out the three hags for a second set of prophecies that Shakespeare's design with equivocation and the interplay of times and places comes into its most dramatic focus. After hearing the riddles, Macbeth witnesses the 'show of eight Kings' from Banquo's line. They form a procession that leads prophetically offstage to the royal audience they will culminate in, and the last of them holds a glass in his hand, presumably to catch the countenance of the King. Genealogy and prophecy are made manifest in a visible display, but there is another genealogy in the air as well, one heard rather than seen. Juxtaposed to the projection of James's line, the witches' riddles complicate its complimentary gesture with what amounts to a genealogy of treason and equivocation: the equivocation the audience knows, defined by James as treason's dissembling lie, has been contextualised or traced back to the less than reassuring figure of treason and rebellion we have been charting in this essay.

Amphibology marks an aspect of language that neither treason nor authority can control. It is a power that cannot be trammelled up, mastered, or unequivocally defined, but it is a power: it compels and moves the speaker or auditor. From the perspective of authority, it does so illicitly – that is, in the place of authority and laws of State, reason, or sense. It is not when Macbeth lies but when the language he would use instead masters him that the power of amphibology strikes us, and its effects are not confined to the witches' riddles.

Language behaves strangely and impulsively in the play, as if with a will of its own. At times Macbeth seems to stride the blast of his own tongue, not so much speaking as he is spoken by his words and their insistent associations. A submerged current propels his speech even when Macbeth dissembles, and it surfaces during his description of the murdered Duncan in the form of a disassembled pun:

> ... his gash'd stabs look'd like a breach in nature
> For ruin's wasteful entrance: there, the murtherers
> Steeped in the colour of their trade, their daggers
> Unmannerly breech'd with gore.
>
> (II.iii.113)

The breach that is an opening in Duncan's flesh – allowing what is outside to intrude, spilling all that should remain within – returns to the mind's eye and ear when 'breech'd' succeeds it so closely. The first suggests or prompts the second in something closer to free association than logical progression of thought. Wound and unmannerly covering, the intrusion of the one homonym upon the other acts as a pun often does, making visualisation of an image difficult. The breeches of gore are themselves breached: one image haunts the other, and we are uncertain which way to take.

With the amphibolic riddle, taking one course through it does not eliminate the other; in his own moving and self-persuading language, Macbeth relies and rides upon gliding significations of words, often with a powerful effect. Authority can either watch and listen to such motions, or it can engage them. In *Macbeth*, Shakespeare develops an unsettling affiliation between treason's spectacle and its audience. To engage treason's motions is to participate in them, threatening the otherwise clear antithesis that would seem to hold between rule and misrule and revealing the latter to be less the antithesis of rule than its alternating current, its overextension and in a sense its consequence. In England with Macduff, Malcolm dissembles. He lies about his own character and tarnishes his reputation, confident that when the test of his compatriot has been made he can remove this mask of misrule as easily as he donned it. But once on his face, it leaves a lasting impression. For Macduff the experience is a discomposing one, for it reveals a family resemblance between authority and its other where no relation was expected. When Malcolm strips away the mask and swears, 'My first false speaking / Was this upon myself' (IV.iii.130), Macduff hesitates, uncertain whether it is Malcolm honest and pure or Malcolm profligate who declares such an absolute division between his lies and his truths. The line he draws and the need to draw it are equally difficult for Macduff to align with his notions of a true ruler: 'Such welcome and unwelcome things at once / 'Tis hard to reconcile' (IV.iii.138).

The words could have been spoken by Macbeth before Duncan's murder, when still on the heath and wondering how to reconcile the foul and fair tidings of the witches' greetings. Both a metaphor and a pun call for a simultaneous perception of likeness and difference, but unlike a metaphor, a pun cannot be reduced to a simile – as Aristotle said any metaphor could be – in order to clarify the lines of its similitude. Amphibology lies *like* truth: similitude here is reason's dilemma, not its exegetical or legal solution. An interplay of likeness and difference, amphibology is less readily ruled than are the antitheses of authority.

IV

Amphibology belongs to treason's spectacle. What is effaced by the time of treason's orderly procession and meticulous execution under the law is something more than a rhetorical figure or mere wordplay, as we understand such terms today. When amphibology surfaces in histories or on the stage it is accorded a power that is generative rather than controlling or restraining. It is something the traitor gives himself up to, and a part of what is generated out of it is the traitor's arc of rebellion. In his study of the 'uncomic puns' in *Macbeth* – 'breach' could be added to it – Kenneth Muir suggests such puns possess a generative power since lost to dramatic language, but he approaches them strictly within the history of literary language and the stage. Characteristic of Shakespearean drama, most pronounced in *Macbeth* yet absent from the stage after the Restoration, the uncomic pun is a part of what separates Shakespeare's language from ours: 'The Restoration dramatists were admirably lucid, but their use of language was, in the last resort, unimaginative. The banishing of the pun except for comic purposes was the symbol of a radical defect: it was a turning away from the genius of the language.'[13]

Muir's thesis is a striking one, but a part of what separates Shakespeare's language from ours is the (an)aesthetisation that has taken place, when amphibology thus resurfaces as a purely linguistic phenomenon whose significance is both entirely aesthetic and even limited to a single genre. For Puttenham the domain of amphibology and the threat posed by it are considerably broader, as they were for the later seventeenth century – which did more than 'turn away' from its *genius linguae*. Indeed, the age subsequent to Shakespeare brought language under its full and controlled scrutiny, not as a

spectacle but as something to chart, analyse, regulate, and even legis-
late into a clear and ordered discourse. Modern grammars, prose
style, and ideas of translation stem from the efforts of the Royal
Society and others to master language, but the ordering and deployment of discourse is also a phenomenon inseparable from the
creation of the modern State.[14] The consequences for the figure of
the traitor, dramatic and rhetorical, are beyond the bounds of this
essay but relevant to it. What I have called amphibology, Puttenham
also describes as ambiguity. I avoid the more familiar term because
of its familiarity. Ambiguity, too, has enjoyed considerable popular-
ity as an aesthetic phenomenon in this century. What the Latin fails
to suggest – partly in its etymology, but more importantly in its
modern usage – is the unruly but generative force associated with
treason's figure. But the Greek term *becomes* unfamiliar. Its strangeness is an historical occurrence, and it seems more than a coincidence
of history or philology that it is during the seventeenth century when
it begins to decline in usage and gives way to the familiar but
relatively pallid 'ambiguity'.

 ... At the opening of the play, in the recounted deaths of
Macdonwald and Cawdor, we encountered differing versions of
treason's last act and final performance; at its close, the play returns
to the question of treason's proper public representation, and from
that question derives its penultimate dramatic impetus. Macbeth has
run his bloody course and stands undone yet no longer deluded,
facing Macduff but hesitant to engage with his doom. Macduff goads
his rival into action with a reminder that treason has another stage
available to it, if it refuses to go the way of a Macdonwald or a
Cawdor:

> Then yield thee, coward
> And live to be the show and gaze o' th' time:
> We'll have thee, as our rarer monsters are,
> Painted upon a pole, and underwrit,
> 'Here you may see the tyrant.'
> (V.viii.23)

Macduff threatens a life in captivity and a gallows procession which,
staged in effigy, can be infinitely repeated – viewed and reviewed by
Macbeth himself, among others. Macbeth is threatened, in a vertigi-
nous sense, with a reduced, silent, purely spectacular version of
Macbeth itself; he chooses instead to die in renewed rebellion. When
he exits it is as a warrior and a traitor, in arms. Macduff returns,
bearing his head, and the traitor is no more.

Yet the entrance of Macbeth's head has a complex effect in a play that has so closely followed and adapted itself to treason's amphibolic course. For a brief time, the figure of the traitor has merged with the figures of Shakespearean language and dramaturgy. For the duration of the play, we are taken beyond James's reduced notion of equivocation as a mere lie and introduced to the realm he was attempting to redefine: a realm less easily governed by the reigning absolutes of Jacobean England, historically occupied by figures of sedition, here taken over by the dramatic and rhetorical figures of Shakespearean dramaturgy. The impulsive power of treason's tongue is a heightened and elaborated version of Shakespeare's language. Macbeth speaks and is propelled by words that lie like truth, and also like Shakespeare at the height of his powers. But the incongruous kinship that develops between the figures of the stage and those of treason is a restricted one. Macbeth's death marks the point where stage and treason must diverge, and his disembodied head crystallises their divergence. To the audience the visage is a familiar one, but it is also out of place, proper to a different setting, customarily viewed on a different scaffold. Macbeth's head in a sense doubles the stage it bloodies, such that we end in a visual representation of the verbal pun: one scaffold portrayed upon the boards of the other, in a closing reformation of treason's spectacle.

From Steven Mullaney, *The Place of the Stage* (Chicago, 1988). The author has kindly supplied a shortened version of chapter 5 of his book.

NOTES

[New Historicism is concerned with the relations between text and historical context, and characteristically these are found to be teasing and complex. Steven Mullaney relates the treachery in *Macbeth* to conspiracies against King James, finding that the equivocal language of the traitor permeates this play, as the traitor both abuses words and is abused by them. *Macbeth* is quoted from Kenneth Muir's New Arden edition (London, 1951). Ed.]

1. *Gowries Conspiracy* (1600), printed in *The Harleian Miscellany* (London, 1808), II, 345.

2. John Nichols, *The Progresses . . . of James the First* (London, 1828), II, 38–43.

3. *The King's Booke* (1605), cited in Henry N. Paul, *The Royal Play of 'Macbeth'* (New York, 1950), p. 230.

4. In Raphael Holinshed, *Chronicles of England, Scotland and Ireland* (1580?; London, 1807–8), III, 1009. Cheeke is included in full by Holinshed, pp. 987–1011.

5. Ibid., p. 985.

6. George Puttenham, *The Arte of English Poesie* (1589; Westminster, 1895), p. 267.

7. Frederic W. Russell, *Kett's Rebellion in Norfolk* (London, 1859), p. 142.

8. Ibid., p. 142.

9. Abraham Fraunce, *The Lawyers Logicke* (1588; Menston 1969), p. 27.

10. See Paul, *The Royal Play*, pp. 226–48.

11. See the entry under 'Mental Reservation' in *The Catholic Encyclopedia*.

12. *The Jesuits Downefall*, cited in Frank L. Huntley, '*Macbeth* and the Background of Jesuitical Equivocation', *PMLA*, 79 (1964), 400, n.45.

13. Kenneth Muir, 'The Uncomic Pun', *Cambridge Journal*, 3 (1950), 484.

14. See R. F. Jones, 'Science and English Prose Style in the Third Quarter of the Seventeenth Century', in *Seventeenth-Century Prose*, ed. S. E. Fish (New York, 1971), pp. 53–90; and Michel Foucault, *The Order of Things* (New York, 1971), pp. 78–208.

10

'Macbeth': History, Ideology and Intellectuals

ALAN SINFIELD

It is often said that Macbeth is about 'evil', but we might draw a more careful distinction: between the violence which the State considers legitimate and that which it does not. Macbeth, we may agree, is a dreadful murderer when he kills Duncan. But when he kills Macdonwald – 'a rebel' (I.ii.10) – he has Duncan's approval:

> For brave Macbeth (well he deserves that name),
> Disdaining Fortune, with his brandish'd steel,
> Which smok'd with bloody execution,
> Like Valour's minion, carv'd out his passage,
> Till he fac'd the slave;
> Which ne'er shook hands, nor bade farewell to him,
> Till he unseam'd him from the nave to th' chops,
> And fix'd his head upon our battlements.
> **Duncan**   O valiant cousin! worthy gentleman!
> (I.ii.16–24)

Violence is good, in this view, when it is in the service of the prevailing dispositions of power; when it disrupts them it is evil. A claim to a monopoly of legitimate violence is fundamental in the development of the modern State; when that claim is successful, most citizens learn to regard State violence as qualitatively different from other violence and perhaps they don't think of State violence as violence at all (consider the actions of police, army and judiciary as opposed to those of pickets, protesters, criminals and terrorists).

Macbeth focuses major strategies by which the State asserted its claim at one conjuncture.

Generally in Europe in the sixteenth century the development was from Feudalism to the Absolutist State. Under Feudalism, the king held authority among his peers, his equals, and his power was often little more than nominal; authority was distributed also among overlapping non-national institutions such as the church, estates, assemblies, regions and towns. In the Absolutist State, power became centralised in the figure of the monarch, the exclusive source of legitimacy. The movement from one to the other was of course contested, not only by the aristocracy and the peasantry, whose traditional rights were threatened, but also by the gentry and urban bourgeoisie, who found new space for power and influence within more elaborate economic and governmental structures. Because of these latter factors especially, the Absolutist State was never fully established in England. Probably the peak of the monarch's personal power was reached by Henry VIII; the attempt of Charles I to reassert that power led to the English Revolution. In between, Elizabeth and James I, and those who believed their interests to lie in the same direction, sought to sustain royal power and to suppress dissidents. The latter category was broad; it comprised aristocrats like the Earls of Northumberland and Westmorland who led the Northern Rising of 1569 and the Duke of Norfolk who plotted to replace Elizabeth with Mary Queen of Scots in 1571, clergy who refused the State religion, gentry who supported them and who tried to raise awkward matters in Parliament, writers and printers who published criticism of State policy, the populace when it complained about food prices, enclosures, or anything.

The exercise of State violence against such dissidents depended upon the achievement of a degree of legitimation – upon the acceptance by many people that State power was, at least, the lesser of two evils. A principal means by which this was effected was the propagation of an ideology of Absolutism, which represented the English State as a pyramid, any disturbance of which would produce general disaster, and which insisted increasingly on the 'divine right' of the monarch. This system was said to be 'natural' and ordained by 'God'; it was 'good' and disruptions of it 'evil'. This is what some Shakespeareans have celebrated as a just and harmonious 'world picture'. ...

The reason why the State needed violence and propaganda was that the system was subject to persistent structural difficulties.

Macbeth, like very many plays of the period, handles anxieties about the violence exercised under the aegis of Absolutist ideology. Two main issues come into focus. The first is the threat of a split between legitimacy and actual power – when the monarch is not the strongest person in the State. Such a split was altogether likely during the transition from Feudalism to the Absolutist State; hence the in-fighting within the dominant group in most European countries. In England the matter was topical because of the Essex rebellion in 1599: it was easy for the charismatic earl, who had shown at Cadiz that Englishmen could defeat Spaniards, to suppose that he would make a better ruler than the ageing and indecisive Elizabeth, for all her legitimacy. So Shakespeare's Richard II warns Northumberland, the kingmaker, that he is bound, structurally, to disturb the rule of Bolingbroke:

> thou shalt think,
> Though he [Bolingbroke] divide the realm and give thee half,
> It is too little, helping him to all.[1]

Jonathan Dollimore and I have argued elsewhere that the potency of the myth of Henry V in Shakespeare's play, written at the time of Essex's ascendancy, derives from the striking combination in that monarch of legitimacy and actual power.[2] At the start of *Macbeth* the manifest dependency of Duncan's State upon its best fighter sets up a dangerous instability (this is explicit in the sources). In the opening soliloquy of Act I scene vii Macbeth freely accords to Duncan entire legitimacy: he is Duncan's kinsman, subject and host, the king has been 'clear in his great office', and the idea of his deposition evokes religious imagery of angels, damnation and cherubins. But that is all the power the king has that does not depend upon Macbeth; against it is ranged 'Vaulting ambition', Macbeth's impetus to convert his actual power into full regal authority.

The split between legitimacy and actual power was always a potential malfunction in the developing Absolutist State. A second problem was less dramatic but more persistent. It was this: what is the difference between Absolutism and tyranny? – having in mind contemporary state violence such as the Massacre of St Bartholomew's in France in 1572, the arrest of more than a hundred witches and the torturing and killing of many of them in Scotland in 1590–91, and the suppression of the Irish by English armies. The immediate reference for questions of legitimate violence in relation to

Macbeth is the Gunpowder Plot of 1605. This attempted violence against the State followed upon many years of State violence against Roman Catholics: the Absolutist State sought to draw religious institutions entirely within its control, and Catholics who actively refused were subjected to fines, imprisonment, torture and execution. Consider the sentence passed upon Jane Wiseman in 1598:

> The sentence is that the said Jane Wiseman shall be led to the prison of the Marshalsea of the Queen's Bench, and there naked, except for a linen cloth about the lower part of her body, be laid upon the ground, lying directly on her back: and a hollow shall be made under her head and her head placed in the same; and upon her body in every part let there be placed as much of stones and iron as she can bear and more; and as long as she shall live, she shall have of the worst bread and water of the prison next her; and on the day she eats, she shall not drink, and on the day she drinks she shall not eat, so living until she die.[3]

This was for 'receiving, comforting, helping and maintaining priests', and refusing to reveal, under torture, who else was doing the same thing, and for refusing to plead. There is nothing abstract or theoretical about the State violence to which the present essay refers. Putting the issue succinctly in relation to Shakespeare's play, what is the difference between Macbeth's rule and that of contemporary European monarchs?

In *Basilikon Doron* (1599) King James tried to protect the Absolutist State from such pertinent questions by asserting an utter distinction between 'a lawfull good King' and 'an usurping Tyran':

> The one acknowledgeth himselfe ordained for his people, having received from God a burthen of government, whereof he must be countable: the other thinketh his people ordeined for him, a prey to his passions and inordinate appetites, as the fruites of his magnanimitie: And therefore, as their ends are directly contrarie, so are their whole actions, as meanes, whereby they preasse to attaine to their endes.[4]

Evidently James means to deny that the Absolutist monarch has anything significant in common with someone like Macbeth. Three aspects of James's strategy in this passage are particularly revealing. First, he depends upon an utter polarisation between the two kinds of ruler. Such antitheses are characteristic of the ideology of Absolutism: they were called upon to tidy the uneven apparatus of Feudal power into a far neater structure of the monarch versus the rest, and protestantism tended to see 'spiritual' identities in similarly polarised terms. James himself explained the function of demons like this: 'since the Devill is the verie contrarie opposite to God, there can be no better way to know God, then by the contrarie'.[5] So it is with the two kinds of rulers: the badness of one seems to guarantee the goodness of the other. Second, by defining the lawful good king against the usurping tyrant, James refuses to admit the possibility that a ruler who has *not* usurped will be tyrannical. Thus he seems to cope with potential splits between legitimacy and actual power by insisting on the unique status of the lawful good king, and to head off questions about the violence committed by such a ruler by suggesting that all his actions will be uniquely legitimate. Third, we may notice that the whole distinction, as James develops it, is in terms not of the *behaviour* of the lawful good king and the usurping tyrant, respectively, but in terms of their *motives*. This seems to render vain any assessment of the actual manner of rule of the Absolute monarch. On these arguments, any disturbance of the current structure of power relations is against God and the people, and consequently any violence in the interest of the status quo is acceptable. Hence the legitimate killing of Jane Wiseman. ...

It is often assumed that *Macbeth* is engaged in the same project as King James: attempting to render coherent and persuasive the ideology of the Absolutist State. The grounds for a Jamesian reading are plain enough – to the point where it is often claimed that the play was designed specially for the king. At every opportunity Macbeth is disqualified ideologically and his opponents ratified. An entire antithetical apparatus of nature and supernature – the concepts through which a dominant ideology most commonly seeks to establish itself – is called upon to witness against him as usurping tyrant. ... The whole strategy is epitomised in the account of Edward's alleged curing of 'the Evil' – actually scrofula – 'A most miraculous work in this good King' (IV.iii.146–7). James himself knew that this was a superstitious practice, and he refused to undertake it until his advisers persuaded him that it would strengthen his claim to the throne in the public eye. As Francis Bacon observed, notions of the supernatural help to keep people acquiescent (e.g. the man in pursuit of power will do well to attribute his success 'rather to divine Providence and felicity, than to his own virtue or policy').[6] *Macbeth* draws upon such notions more than any other play by Shakespeare. It all suggests that Macbeth is an extraordinary eruption in a good State – obscuring the thought that there might be any pronity to structural malfunctioning in the system. It suggests that Macbeth's

violence is wholly bad, whereas State violence committed by legitimate monarchs is quite different.

Such manoeuvres are even more necessary to a Jamesian reading of
the play in respect of the deposition and killing of Macbeth.
Absolutist ideology declared that even tyrannical monarchs must not
be resisted, yet Macbeth could hardly be allowed to triumph. Here
the play offers two moves. First, the fall of Macbeth seems to result
more from (super)natural than human agency: it seems like an effect
of the opposition of good and evil ('Macbeth / Is ripe for shaking,
and the Powers above / Put on their instruments' – IV.iii.237–9).
Most cunningly, although there are material explanations for the
moving of Birnam Wood and the unusual birth of Macduff, the
audience is allowed to believe, at the same time, that these are
(super)natural effects (thus the play works upon us almost as the
Witches work upon Macbeth). Second, in so far as Macbeth's fall is
accomplished by human agency, the play is careful to suggest that he
is hardly in office before he is overthrown. The years of successful
rule specified in the chronicles are erased and, as Paul points out,
neither Macduff nor Malcolm has tendered any allegiance to
Macbeth.[7] The action rushes along, he is swept away as if he had
never truly been king. *Even so*, the contradiction can hardly vanish
altogether. For the Jamesian reading it is necessary for Macbeth to be
a complete usurping tyrant in order that he shall set off the lawful
good king, and also, at the same time, for him not to be a ruler at all
in order that he may properly be deposed and killed. Macbeth kills
two people at the start of the play: a rebel and the king, and these are
apparently utterly different acts of violence. That is the ideology of
Absolutism. Macduff also, killing Macbeth, is killing both a rebel
and a king, but now the two are apparently the same person. The
ultimate intractability of this kind of contradiction disturbs the
Jamesian reading of the play.

Criticism has often supposed, all too easily, that the Jamesian
reading of *Macbeth* is necessary on historical grounds – that other
views of State ideology were impossible for Shakespeare and his
contemporaries. But this was far from being so: there was a well-
developed theory allowing for resistance by the nobility, and the
Gunpowder Plotters were manifestly unconvinced by the king's
arguments. Even more pertinent is the theory of the Scotsman
George Buchanan, as we may deduce from the fact that James tried
to suppress Buchanan's writings in 1584 after his assumption of

personal rule; in *Basilikon Doron* he advises his son to 'use the Law upon the keepers' of 'such infamous invectives' (p. 40). With any case so strenuously overstated and manipulative as James's, we should ask what alternative position it is trying to put down. Arguments in favour of Absolutism constitute one part of *Macbeth*'s ideological field – the range of ideas and attitudes brought into play by the text; another main part may be represented by Buchanan's *De jure regni* (1579) and *History of Scotland* (1582). In Buchanan's view sovereignty derives from and remains with the people; the king who exercises power against their will is a tyrant and should be deposed. The problem in Scotland is not unruly subjects, but unruly monarchs: 'Rebellions there spring less from the people than from the rulers, when they try to reduce a kingdom which from earliest times had always been ruled by law to an absolute and lawless despotism'.[8] Buchanan's theory is the virtual antithesis of James's; it was used eventually to justify the deposition of James's son.

Buchanan's *History of Scotland* is usually reckoned to be one of the sources of *Macbeth*. It was written to illustrate his theory of sovereignty and to justify the overthrow of Mary Queen of Scots in 1567. In it the dichotomy of true lawful king and usurping tyrant collapses, for Mary is the lawful ruler *and* the tyrant, and her deposers are usurpers *and yet* lawful also. To her are attributed many of the traits of Macbeth: she is said to hate integrity in others, to appeal to the predictions of witches, to use foreign mercenaries, to place spies in the households of opponents and to threaten the lives of the nobility; after her surrender she is humiliated in the streets of Edinburgh as Macbeth fears to be. It is alleged that she would not have shrunk from the murder of her son if she could have reached him. This account of Mary as arch-tyrant embarrassed James, and that is perhaps why just eight kings are shown to Macbeth by the Witches (IV.i.119). Nevertheless, it was well established in protestant propaganda and in Spenser's *Faerie Queene*, and the Gunpowder Plot would tend to revivify it. Any recollection of the alleged tyranny of Mary, the lawful ruler, prompts awareness of the contradictions in Absolutist ideology, disturbing the customary interpretation of *Macbeth*. Once we are alert to this disturbance, the Jamesian reading of the play begins to leak at every joint. ... Duncan's status is in doubt: it is unclear how far his authority runs, he is imperceptive, and his State is in chaos well before Macbeth's violence against it (G. K. Hunter in the introduction to his Penguin edition [1967] registers unease at the 'violence and bloodthirstiness' of Macbeth's killing of Macdonwald [pp. 9–10]). Nor is Malcolm's title altogether clear, since Duncan's declaration of him as 'Prince of Cumberland' (I.iv.35–42) suggests what the chronicles indicate, namely that the succession was not necessarily hereditary; Macbeth seems to be elected by the thanes (II.iv.29–32).

I have suggested that *Macbeth* may be read as working to justify the overthrow of the usurping tyrant. Nevertheless, the *awkwardness* of the issue is brought to the surface by the uncertain behaviour of Banquo. In the sources he collaborates with Macbeth, but to allow that in the play would taint King James's line and blur the idea of the one monstrous eruption. Shakespeare compromises and makes Banquo do nothing at all. He fears Macbeth played 'most foully for't' (III.i.3) but does not even communicate his knowledge of the Witches' prophecies. Instead he wonders if they may 'set me up in hope' (III.i.10). If it is right for Malcolm and Macduff, eventually, to overthrow Macbeth, then it would surely be right for Banquo to take a clearer line.

Furthermore, the final position of Macduff appears quite disconcerting, once we read it with Buchanan's more realistic, political analysis in mind: Macduff at the end stands in the same relation to Malcolm as Macbeth did to Duncan in the beginning. He is now the king-maker on whom the legitimate monarch depends, and the recurrence of the whole sequence may be anticipated (in production this might be suggested by a final meeting of Macduff and the Witches). For the Jamesian reading it is necessary to feel that Macbeth is a distinctively 'evil' eruption in a 'good' system; awareness of the role of Macduff in Malcolm's State alerts us to the fundamental instability of power relations during the transition to Absolutism, and consequently to the uncertain validity of the claim of the State to the legitimate use of violence. Certainly Macbeth is a murderer and an oppressive ruler, but he is one version of the Absolutist ruler, not the polar opposite.

Malcolm himself raises very relevant issues in the conversation in which he tests Macduff: specifically tyrannical qualities are invoked. At one point, according to Buchanan, the Scottish lords 'give the benefit of the doubt' to Mary and her husband, following the thought that 'more secret faults' may be tolerated 'so long as these do not involve a threat to the welfare of the state'.[9] Macduff is prepared to accept considerable threats to the welfare of Scotland:

> Boundless intemperance
> In nature is a tyranny; it hath been
> Th' untimely emptying of the happy throne,
> And fall of many kings. But fear not yet
> To take upon you what is yours: you may
> Convey your pleasures in a spacious plenty,
> And yet seem cold – the time you may so hoodwink:
> We have willing dames enough; there cannot be
> That vulture in you, to devour so many
> As will to greatness dedicate themselves,
> Finding it so inclin'd.
>
> (IV.iii.66–76)

Tyranny in nature means disturbance in the metaphorical kingdom of a person's nature but, in the present context, one is likely to think of the effects of the monarch's intemperance on the literal kingdom. Macduff suggests that such behaviour has caused the fall not just of usurpers but of kings, occupants of 'the happy throne'. Despite this danger, he encourages Malcolm 'To take upon you what is yours' – a sinister way of putting it, implying either Malcolm's title to the State in general or his rights over the women he wants to seduce or assault. Fortunately the latter will not be necessary, there are 'willing dames enough': Macduff is ready to mortgage both the bodies and (within the ideology invoked in the play) the souls of women to the monster envisaged as lawful good king. It will be all right, apparently, because people can be hoodwinked: Macduff allows us to see that the virtues James tries to identify with the Absolutist monarch are an ideological strategy, and that the illusion of them will probably be sufficient to keep the system going.

Nor is this the worst: Malcolm claims more faults, and according to Macduff 'avarice / Sticks deeper' (lines 84–5): Malcolm may corrupt not merely people but property relations. Yet this too is to be condoned. Of course, Malcolm is not actually like this, but the point is that he well could be, as Macduff says many kings have been, and that would all be acceptable. And even Malcolm's eventual protestation of innocence cannot get round the fact that he has been lying. He says 'my first false speaking / Was this upon myself' (lines 130–1) and that may indeed be true, but it nevertheless indicates the circumspection that will prove useful to the lawful good king, as much as to the tyrant. In Holinshed the culminating vice claimed by Malcolm is lying, but Shakespeare replaces it with a general and rather desperate evocation of utter tyranny (lines 91–100); was the original self-accusation perhaps too pointed? The whole conversation takes off from the specific and incomparable tyranny of Macbeth, but in the process succeeds in suggesting that there may be considerable overlap between the qualities of the tyrant and the true king.

Macbeth allows space for two quite different interpretive organisations: against a Jamesian illustration of the virtues of Absolutism we may produce a disturbance of that reading, illuminated by Buchanan. This latter makes visible the way religion is used to underpin State ideology, and undermines notions that established monarchs must not be challenged or removed and that State violence is utterly distinctive and legitimate. It is commonly assumed that the function of criticism is to resolve such questions of interpretation – to go through the text with an eye to sources, other plays, theatrical convention, historical context and so on, deciding on which side the play comes down and explaining away contrary evidence. However, this is neither an adequate programme nor an adequate account of what generally happens.

Let us suppose, to keep the argument moving along, that the Jamesian reading fits better with *Macbeth* and its Jacobean context, as we understand them at present. Two questions then present themselves: what is the status of the disturbance of that reading, which I have produced by bringing Buchanan into view? And what are the consequences of customary critical insistence upon the Jamesian reading?

On the first question, I would make three points. First, the Buchanan disturbance *is in the play*, and inevitably so. Even if we believe that Shakespeare was trying to smooth over difficulties in Absolutist ideology, to do this significantly he must deal with the issues which resist convenient inclusion. Those issues must be brought into visibility in order that they can be handled, and once exposed they are available for the reader or audience to seize and focus upon, as an alternative to the more complacent reading. A position tends to suppose an *op*position. Even James's writings are vulnerable to such analysis, for instance when he brings up the awkward fact that the prophet Samuel urgently warns the people of Israel against choosing a king because he will tyrannise over them. This prominent biblical instance could hardly be ignored, so James quotes it and says that Samuel was preparing the Israelites to be obedient and patient.[10] Yet once James has brought Samuel's pronouncement into visibility, the reader is at liberty to doubt the king's tendentious interpretation of it. It is hardly possible to deny the reader this scope: even the most strenuous closure can be repudiated as inadequate. We are led to think of the text not as propounding a unitary and coherent meaning which is to be discovered, but as handling a range of issues (probably intractable issues, for they make the best stories), and as unable to control the development of radically divergent interpretations.

Second, the Buchanan disturbance has been activated, in the present essay, as a consequence of the writer's scepticism about Jamesian ideological strategies and his concern with current political issues. It is conceivable that many readers of *Macbeth* will come to share this outlook. Whether this happens or not, the theoretical implication may be taken: if such a situation should come about, the terms in which *Macbeth* is customarily discussed would shift, and eventually the Buchanan disturbance would come to seem an obvious, natural way to consider the play. That is how notions of appropriate approaches to a text get established. We may observe the process, briefly, in the career of the Witches. For many members of Jacobean audiences, Witches were a social and spiritual reality: they were as real as Edward the Confessor, perhaps more so. As belief in the physical manifestation of supernatural powers, and especially demonic powers, weakened, the Witches were turned into an operatic display, with new scenes, singing and dancing, fine costumes and flying machines. In an adaptation by Sir William Davenant, this was the only stage form of the play from 1674 to 1744, and even after Davenant's version was abandoned the Witches' divertissements were staged, until 1888. Latterly we have adopted other ways with the Witches – being still unable, of course, to contemplate them, as most of Shakespeare's audience probably did, as phenomena one might encounter on a heath. Kenneth Muir comments: 'with the fading of belief in the objective existence of devils, they and their operations can yet symbolize the workings of evil in the hearts of men'.[11] Recent critical accounts and theatrical productions have developed all kinds of strategies to make the Witches 'work' for our time. These successive accommodations of one aspect of the play to prevailing attitudes are blatant, but they illustrate the extent to which critical orthodoxy is not the mere response to the text which it claims to be: it is *remaking* it within currently acceptable parameters. The Buchanan disturbance may not always remain a marginal gloss to the Jamesian reading.

Third, we may assume that the Buchanan disturbance was part of the response of some among the play's initial audiences. It is in the nature of the matter that it is impossible to assess how many people inclined towards Buchanan's analysis of royal power. That there were such may be supposed from the multifarious challenges to State authority – culminating, of course, in the Civil War. *Macbeth* was almost certainly read against James by some Jacobeans. This destroys the claim to privilege of the Jamesian reading on the ground that it is historically valid: we must envisage diverse original audiences, activating diverse implications in the text. And we may demand comparable interpretive license for ourselves. Initially the play occupied a complex position in its ideological field, and we should expect no less today.

With these considerations about the status of the Buchanan disturbance in mind, the question about the customary insistence on the Jamesian reading appears as a question about the politics of criticism. Like other kinds of cultural production, literary criticism helps to influence the way people think about the world; that is why the present essay seeks to make space for an oppositional understanding of the text and the State. It is plain that most criticism has not only reproduced but endorsed Jamesian ideology, so discouraging scrutiny, which *Macbeth* can promote, of the legitimacy of State violence. That we are dealing with live issues is shown by the almost uncanny resemblances between the Gunpowder Plot and the bombing in 1984 by the Irish Republican Army of the Brighton hotel where leading members of the government were staying, and in the comparable questions about State and other violence which they raise. My concluding thoughts are about the politics of the prevailing readings of *Macbeth*. I distinguish conservative and liberal positions; both tend to dignify their accounts with the honorific term 'tragedy'.

The conservative position insists that the play is about 'evil'. . . . Often this view is elaborated as a socio-political programme, allegedly expounded by Shakespeare and implicitly endorsed by the critic. So Muir writes of 'an orderly and closely-knit society, in contrast to the disorder consequent upon Macbeth's initial crime [i.e. killing Duncan, not Macdonwald]. The naturalness of that order, and the unnaturalness of its violation by Macbeth, is emphasized . . .' (New Arden *Macbeth*, p. li). Irving Ribner says Fleance is 'symbolic of a future rooted in the acceptance of natural law, which inevitably must return to reassert God's harmonious order when evil has worked itself out'.[12]

This conservative endorsement of Jamesian ideology is not intended to ratify the Modern State. Rather, like much twentieth-century literary criticism, it is backward-looking, appealing to an earlier and preferable supposed condition of society. Roger Scruton comments: 'If a conservative is also a restorationist, this is because he lives close to society, and feels in himself the sickness which infects the common order. How, then, can he fail to direct his eyes towards that state of health from which things have declined?'[13] This quotation is close to the terms in which many critics write of *Macbeth*, and their evocation of the Jamesian order which is allegedly restored at the end of the play constitutes a wistful gesture towards what they would regard as a happy ending for our troubled society. However, because this conservative approach is based on an inadequate analysis of political and social process, it gains no purchase on the main determinants of State power.

A liberal position hesitates to endorse any State power so directly, finding some saving virtue in Macbeth: 'To the end he never totally loses our sympathy'; 'we must still not lose our sympathy for the criminal'.[14] In this view there is a flaw in the State, it fails to accommodate the particular consciousness of the refined individual. Macbeth's imagination is set against the blandness of normative convention and for all his transgressions, perhaps because of them, Macbeth transcends the laws he breaks. In John Bayley's version: 'His superiority consists in a passionate sense for ordinary life, its seasons and priorities, a sense which his fellows in the play ignore in themselves or take for granted. Through the deed which tragedy requires of him he comes to know not only himself, but what life is all about.'[15] I call this 'liberal' because it is anxious about a State, Absolutist or Modern, which can hardly take cognisance of the individual sensibility, and it is prepared to validate to some degree the recalcitrant individual. But it will not undertake the political analysis which would press the case. Hence there is always in such criticism a reservation about Macbeth's revolt and a sense of relief that it ends in defeat: nothing could have been done anyway, it was all inevitable, written in the human condition. This retreat from the possibility of political analysis and action leaves the State virtually unquestioned, almost as fully as the conservative interpretation.

Shakespeare, notoriously, has a way of anticipating all possibilities. The idea of literary intellectuals identifying their own deepest intuitions of the universe in the experience of the 'great' tragic hero who defies the limits of the human condition is surely a little absurd; we may sense delusions of grandeur. *Macbeth* includes much more likely models for its conservative and liberal critics in the characters of the two doctors. The English Doctor has just four and a half lines (IV.iii.141–5) in which he says King Edward is coming and that sick people whose malady conquers the greatest efforts of medical skill await him, expecting a heavenly cure for 'evil'. Malcolm, the king to be, says 'I thank you, Doctor'. This doctor is the equivalent of conservative intellectuals who encourage respect for mystificatory images of ideal hierarchy which have served the State in the past, and who invoke 'evil', 'tragedy' and 'the human condition' to produce, in effect, acquiescence in State power.

The Scottish Doctor, in V.i. and V.iii, is actually invited to cure the sickness of the rulers and by implication the State: 'If thou couldst, Doctor, cast / The water of my land, find her disease . . .' (V.iii.50–1). But this doctor, like the liberal intellectual, hesitates to press an analysis. He says: 'This disease is beyond my practice' (V.i.56), 'I think, but dare not speak' (V.i.76), 'Therein the patient / Must minister to himself' (V.iii.45–6), 'Were I from Dunsinane away and clear, / Profit again should hardly draw me here' (V.iii.61–2). He wrings his hands at the evidence of State violence and protects his conscience with asides. This is like the liberal intellectual who knows there is something wrong at the heart of the system but will not envisage a radical alternative and, to ratify this attitude, discovers in Shakespeare's plays 'tragedy' and 'the human condition' as explanations of the supposedly inevitable defeat of the person who steps out of line.

By conventional standards, the present essay is perverse. But an oppositional criticism is bound to appear thus: its task is to work across the grain of customary assumptions and, if necessary, across the grain of the text, as it is customarily perceived. Of course, literary intellectuals don't have much influence over State violence, their therapeutic power is very limited. Nevertheless, writing, teaching, and other modes of communicating all contribute to the steady, long-term formation of opinion, to the establishment of legitimacy. This contribution King James himself did not neglect. An oppositional analysis of texts like *Macbeth* will read them to expose, rather than promote, State ideologies.

From *Critical Quarterly*, 28, nos. 1, 2 (1986), 63–77.

NOTES

[This extract considers the ideological pressures which tend to produce Macbeth as a uniquely 'evil' figure, and whether his actions might better be understood in terms of the political structures of early-modern Britain. The further issue then (as elsewhere in this volume) is the status of such divergent readings. In a typically cultural-materialist conclusion, the essay addresses the politics of such readings today. *Macbeth* is quoted from the ninth New Arden edition, ed. Kenneth Muir (London, 1962). Ed.]

1. *King Richard II*, ed. Peter Ure, New Arden edition (London, 1956), V.i.59–61.

2. Jonathan Dollimore and Alan Sinfield, 'History and Ideology: the Instance of *Henry V*', in *Alternative Shakespeares*, ed. John Drakakis (London, 1985).

3. John Gerard, *The Autobiography of an Elizabethan*, trans. Philip Caraman (London, 1951), pp. 52–3.

4. *Basilikon Doron*, in *The Political Works of James I*, ed. Charles H. McIlwain (New York, 1965), p. 18.

5. King James the First, *Demonologie (1597), Newes from Scotland (1591)* (London, 1924), p. 55.

6. Francis Bacon, *Essays*, intr. Michael J. Hawkins (London, 1972), p. 160.

7. Henry N. Paul, *The Royal Play of 'Macbeth'* (New York, 1950), p. 196.

8. *The Tyrannous Reign of Mary Stewart, George Buchanan's Account*, trans. and ed. W. A. Gatherer (Edinburgh, 1958), p. 49.

9. Ibid., p. 88.

10. *The Trew Law of Free Monarchies*, in *Political Works*, ed. McIlwain, pp. 56–61; referring to I Sam. 8:9–20.

11. Muir (ed.), *Macbeth*, p. lxx.

12. Ibid., p. li; Irving Ribner, *Patterns in Shakespearean Tragedy* (London, 1960), p. 159.

13. Roger Scruton, *The Meaning of Conservatism* (Harmondsworth, 1980), p. 21.

14. A. C. Bradley, *Shakespearean Tragedy*, 2nd edn (London, 1965), p. 305; Wayne Booth, 'Macbeth as Tragic Hero', in *Shakespeare's Tragedies*, ed. Laurence Lerner (Harmondsworth, 1963), p. 186.

15. John Bayley, *Shakespeare and Tragedy* (London, 1981), p. 199.

11

Tragedy and Literature

JONATHAN DOLLIMORE

Central to the development of essentialist humanism is a view of
tragedy which sees it almost exclusively in terms of man's defeated
potential. But it is a kind of defeat which actually confirms the
potential. Perhaps this is the significance of 'tragic waste': the forces
destructive of life (fate, fortune, the gods or whatever) paradoxically
pressure it into its finest expression in the events which lead to, and
especially those which immediately precede, the protagonist's death.
In one sense what is being identified is a potential somehow passively
realised in its very defeat. We see, for example, protagonists learning
wisdom through suffering, willing to know and endure their fate
even as it destroys them. It may be that the individual, in virtue of a
'tragic flaw', is partly responsible for his or her suffering. Even so, the
extent of that suffering is usually disproportionate to the weakness
(hubris, passion, ambition or whatever); to this extent the individual
is more sinned against than sinning, and his or her potential is finally
reaffirmed in a capacity to suffer with more than human fortitude:
'There is grace on mortals who so nobly die'. Additionally the
protagonist's potential may be realised in a sacrificial sense, death
leading to regeneration of the community and, perhaps, of the
universe. ...

In his analysis of Anglo-American literary criticism John Fekete
has identified what he sees as its fundamental preoccupation,
namely:

> A questioning of all forms of objectivity in relation to a *telos* of
> harmonic integration ... The central problematic of the tradition is
> structured by questions of unity and equilibrium, of order and stability.

From the beginning, but increasing systematically, the tradition embraces the 'whole' and structures a totality without struggle and historical movement.[1]

... It is a preoccupation especially apparent in tragedy – no theory of which has been more influential for interpreting the drama of the early seventeenth century than A. C. Bradley's. Rejection of his speculative character analysis in Shakespeare has tended to obscure the extent to which Bradley's metaphysic of tragedy has remained dominant.

Bradley denied that the ultimate power in the tragic universe could be adequately described in terms of Christian providentialism. Nevertheless he insists that such a power does exist, and, in effect, he recuperates the fundamental metaphysical tenets of providentialism in a theory which blends mystical intuition with an etiolated version of the Hegelian dialectic. ... For Hegel, the imperative 'know thyself' concerned not the individual as such but knowledge of 'man's genuine reality – of what is essentially and ultimately true and real – of mind as the true and essential being'.[2] The mind or spirit in question is of course the Hegelian Absolute Spirit, the complexities of which it is unnecessary to enter into here since Bradley's indebtedness to Hegel is tentative, highly qualified and full of a 'painful mystery' all its own. What is important is that Bradley tends to concentrate upon the Hegelian theme of reconciliation rather than that of dialectical process. Moreover he tends to conceive of absolute spirit not in historical but subjective terms (as a function of 'character'). So, in Shakespearean tragedy, a 'conflict of forces in the hero's soul' becomes the focus for the self-division of an ultimately spiritual power.[3] This conflict leads to apotheosis in death: 'In any Shakespearean tragedy we watch some elect spirit colliding, partly through its error and defect, with a superhuman power which bears it down; and yet we feel that this spirit, even in the error and defect, rises by greatness into ideal union with the power that overwhelms it'.[4] The importance of this double emphasis in Bradley – reconciliation rather than dialectical process, 'character' rather than history – could hardly be overestimated: those aspects of Hegelian philosophy which he declined, and those which he took up, are crucial for the development of the materialist and the idealist traditions respectively. ... So for Bradley, tragedy gestures constantly towards – even though it can never fully reveal – an ultimate order of things, an order monistic and mystical, beyond the realm of language, rooted in paradox and accessible only as 'a presentiment, formless but haunting and even profound'. But to the extent that the ultimate force of the tragic universe is on the side of good and antagonistic to evil, it can still be described as moral.[5] Tragedy is a movement through massive cosmic eruption – 'the self division and intestinal warfare of the ethical substance, not so much the war of good with evil as the war of good with good' – to a final Hegelian reconciliation; tragic catastrophe is 'the violent self-restitution of the divided spiritual unity'.[6] Thus even in the bleakest of tragedies, *King Lear*, we are left with neither depression nor despair but 'a sense of law and beauty . . . a consciousness of greatness in pain, and of solemnity in the mystery we cannot fathom'. This sense of tragedy as 'piteous, fearful and mysterious'[7] is something Bradley comes back to time and again.

In Bradley the conceptual apparatus of continental metaphysics is largely dispensed with and the metaphysical truth reconstituted experientially (or pseudo-experientially). Likewise, crucially, with the subsequent critical tradition; as a recent critic of Shakespeare puts it (though making no mention here of Bradley):

> In *Macbeth* . . . the sanctions of divine law become the laws of human consciousness, and the vengeance of God becomes the purgative action of the diseased social organism. [Moreover] the sense of moral order, far from being stunted by this pruning away of the transcendental leafage, merely strikes deeper roots into the soil of consciousness, and grows more compelling as it is less definable.[8]

'Less definable': compare this, and also Bradley's 'mystery that we cannot fathom', with the assurance of Hegel:

> The true course of dramatic development consists in the annulment of contradictions.

> Over and above mere fear and tragic sympathy we have therefore the feeling of *reconciliation*, which tragedy affords in virtue of its vision of eternal justice.

> Eternal justice is operative . . . under a mode whereby it restores the ethical substance and unity in and along with the downfall of the individuality which disturbs its repose.[9]

From those more recent theorists and critics of tragedy who could be cited in support of the contention that Bradley has been, and remains, a powerful influence, three may suffice.

'Tragedy' says Richard B. Sewall, speaks 'of an order that transcends time, space and matter . . . some order behind the immediate disorder.' Like Bradley he is at pains to stress that this is 'nothing so pat as The Moral Order, the "armies of unalterable law", and it is nothing so sure as the orthodox Christian God'. Like Bradley, again, he sees it as much more mystical and mysterious than any of these, involving 'faith in a cosmic good; [a] vision, however fleeting, of a world in which all questions could be answered'.[10] G. K. Hunter has offered a providential account of Elizabethan tragedy which also shows a specific resemblance to Bradley's. Elucidating Fulke Greville's famous account of the difference between ancient and contemporary tragedy Hunter adds that, in the latter, the massacre of innocents 'is part of a larger catastrophic movement which is eventually moral: the universe in casting out the particular evil casts out the good'; compare Bradley's view that the moral order, in making its tragic heroes 'suffer and waste themselves', actually 'suffers and wastes itself; . . . to save its life and regain peace from this intestinal struggle, it casts them out'.[11]

In *Elements of Tragedy* Dorothea Krook, ignoring all historical contexts and differences, posits four 'fundamental, universal elements of tragedy': first an act of shame or horror which violates the moral order, second expiatory suffering, third knowledge of the necessity of that suffering, fourth an affirmation of the dignity of the human spirit, and, in the greatest tragedy, affirmation of a transcendent moral order. Linking these four elements is a principle of teleological coherence:

> The final 'affirmation' of tragedy springs from our reconciliation to, or acceptance of, the necessity of the suffering rendered intelligible by the knowledge: by illuminating the necessity of the suffering the knowledge reconciles us to it; by being reconciled to ('accepting') the suffering as necessary, we reaffirm the supremacy of the universal moral order; and by the act of recognition of and submission to the universal moral order . . . we express and affirm the dignity of man.[12]

The underlying structure of Krook's tragedy is undoubtedly Christian but equally important is the humanist centring of 'man': the tragic hero who suffers into truth 'is all mankind' and represents 'all humanity in embodying some fundamental, persistent aspect of man's nature' (p. 36); the universal qualities of the hero are courage and nobility (p. 41). . . .

In one sense the humanist theory of tragedy repudiates the religious desire to be folded within the absolute; moreover in such tragedy the absolute is typically construed not redemptively but as a force permanently hostile to man's deepest needs. Nevertheless tragic death restores transcendent unity to the subject and to man, not despite but because of the fact that now it ceases to be conditional upon a redemptive identification with the absolute. Man gathers that unity into himself; his essential nature is pressured into its full being. Individual extinction leads to the apotheosis of man, who now becomes his own universal. Further – and this too is a consequence of this view being a displaced theology – suffering and loss are mystified, rendered inevitable and unalterable and, as such, become the pre-condition for instantiation of the universal. John Tinsley has recently (1982) characterised very clearly this tragic sense of life; it always contains, he says, 'a vision of man remaining incomparably superior to all those circumstances which seem only to underline his ultimate insignificance and transitoriness . . . it expresses a solicitude for, and a stoic pride in, man who is the victim of so much pain, and a resentment against the fortuitous character of human calamity and against any God, who, if he exists, must be held to permit this'; further, it replaces ideas of creation and providence with some kind of fatalism. For Tinsley, a bishop, such a view as it stands is of course unacceptable to the Christian faith. But, situated as it is 'equally removed from both faith and despair', it is redeemable.[13]

Bishop Tinsley is quite right: the tragic sense of life as articulated in idealist culture *is* redeemable for Christian faith, and the parameters of his discussion – faith and despair, the tragic and the comic, atonement and redemption, Christian irony, fatalism and reconciliation – indicate why this is so: both perspectives, the tragic and the Christian, remain within the same idealist problematic, one which can be best characterised in terms of what it excludes, namely the single most important concept in materialist analysis: praxis. It is a concept which severs the connection between individuality and man, between subjectivity and the human condition. Consequently it rejects the 'tragic' belief in a human essence which by its own nature as well as its relation to the universal order of things, must inevitably suffer. On the contrary, as Raymond Williams says of Brecht: 'We have to see not only that suffering is avoidable, but that it is not avoided. And not only that suffering breaks us but that it need not break us'.[14] . . .

William Archer's *The Old Drama and the New* appeared in 1923, T. S. Eliot's 'Four Elizabethan Dramatists' in 1924. Archer argued, contentiously, that Elizabethan drama was seriously vitiated by its dependence upon unrealistic conventions. Eliot boldly asserted the contrary: 'The weakness of the Elizabethan drama is not its defect of realism, but its attempt at realism; not its conventions, but its lack of conventions'. This makes the drama an 'impure art' – that is, one which tries to combine 'complete realism' with 'unrealistic conventions'.[15]

For Archer dramatic form simply reflected, unproblematically, the real world – hence his advocacy of a 'pure and consistent form of imitation'.[16] For Eliot also purity of form was an objective of art but one to be achieved through *abstraction* from life rather than direct representation of it – hence his insistence on the importance of conventions and his rejection of realism. It is, says Eliot, 'essential that a work of art should be self-consistent, that an artist should consciously or unconsciously draw a circle beyond which he does not trespass: on the one hand actual life is always the material, and on the other hand an abstraction from actual life is a necessary condition to the creation of the work of art'.[17]

Archer wanted 'realism', Eliot convention. And they wanted different things precisely because they held different conceptions of, first, *reality itself*, second and consequently, what the relationship of art to reality should be. Archer's scathing criticism of the Elizabethans' 'semi-barbarous drama' and his own faith in 'realism' was based on a 'rationalist's' conception of the world and a faith in the correspondence of appearance and reality; for him drama had to imitate 'the visible and audible surfaces of life', to be 'sober and accurate' and in accord with 'common sense'.[18] Further, as Jonas Barish has remarked, for Archer 'everything surprising, contradictory, bewildering in human nature . . . [was] ruled out of court as unnatural'.[19] Eliot saw the world totally differently. In fact, in the very year that Archer's book appeared Eliot had spoken of 'the immense panorama of futility and anarchy which is contemporary history'.[20]

The principal theme of 'Four Elizabethan Dramatists' is that inner consistency is a major criterion of aesthetic achievement; its underlying assumption – one which sheds light on that theme – is that reality is chaotic. Consequently, the aesthetic consistency in question could only be achieved through a careful filtering of reality, followed by adjustment of the selected elements in relation to each other through the use of non-realistic conventions. Occasionally the Jacobean dramatists fulfilled this requirement. Thus Eliot says of *The Revenger's Tragedy* (somewhat oddly), 'the whole action . . . has its own self-subsistent reality';[21] and in *The Sacred Wood*: 'The worlds created by artists like Jonson are like systems of non-Euclidean geometry';[22] interestingly this sentence was omitted from this essay as it appeared later in *Selected Essays*.

To an important extent then art from this perspective becomes formalist – an internally coherent alternative to, rather than a direct representation of, reality; the chaos of the real, the contradictions in experience, are to be excluded rather than, as in Bradley, confronted and transcended in accord with a more ultimate reality. In his essay on Shakespeare and Seneca, Eliot makes a strong distinction between poetry on the one hand and thought, philosophy and intellect on the other. He goes so far as to doubt whether the philosophy of Machiavelli, Montaigne and Seneca could even be said to have influenced Elizabethan writers but, even if it is to be allowed that it did, the influence was not important; so, in Donne for example, he finds 'only a vast jumble of incoherent erudition on which he drew *for purely poetic effects*'. This suggests an even more uncompromising formalism. But Eliot cannot abandon the idea that poetry refers beyond itself and significantly so; thus, although 'In truth neither Shakespeare nor Dante did any real thinking' nevertheless 'the *essential* is that each expresses, in perfect language, some permanent human impulse . . . something *universal* and personal'.[23] By the time of *The Four Quartets* metaphysical and aesthetic significance are re-aligned: 'Only by the form, the pattern / Can words or music reach / The stillness'. Chaos is no longer excluded through unrealistic conventions but transcended through mystical insight into an ultimate reality and articulated now in terms of its appropriate form.

The positions represented by Bradley and Eliot remained central in twentieth-century criticism of Jacobean tragedy; time and again we find the *telos* of harmonic integration as a dominant critical ideal, sometimes in uncompromisingly formalist terms (Eliot) but more usually as an aesthetic reflection of the eternally true, the unchanging human condition (Bradley, later Eliot). In either alternative, history plays no effective part, being either aesthetically/formally excluded or metaphysically transcended. Of course for others in the dominant tradition history *was* deemed important and very much so, but it was still a history filtered through the same ideological imperatives of order. As J. W. Lever has shown in an excellent survey of twentieth-century Shakespearean scholarship, it was this playwright's 'politics' that received most scholarly attention during the years which culminated in the second world war. His alleged conformity to received ideas was constantly proclaimed, ideas which expressed confident belief in order, degree, constituted authority, obedience to rulers and a corresponding contempt for the populace, and so on. In particular, E. M. W. Tillyard extracted from these ideas '*a symmetrical design* whose natural or metaphysical aspects served mainly to justify the social political *status quo*'.[24]

... Bradley and Eliot can be seen to have represented and perpetuated two dominant positions on the question of the relation of art to reality. According to one position aesthetic form was seen to create an ideal unity, a fictive alternative to the chaotic real; according to the other it was seen to represent or invoke an order of truth beyond the flux and chaos of history and be the more 'real' for so doing. ...

Put very schematically, western metaphysics has typically had recourse to three indissociable categories: the universal (or absolute), essence, and teleology. If universals and essences designate, respectively, what ultimately and essentially exists, then teleology designates metaphysical destiny – for the universe as a whole and its essences in particular. ... Anti-humanism, like materialist criticism more generally, challenges the idea that 'man' possesses some given, unalterable essence which is what makes 'him' human, which is the source and *essential* determinant of 'his' culture and its priority over conditions of existence.

It is the Enlightenment rather than the Renaissance which marks the emergence of essentialist humanism as we now know it; at that time concern shifts from the metaphysically derivative soul to what Robert Paul Wolff has termed 'individual centres of consciousness' which are said to be self-determining, free and rational by nature.[25] Those forms of individualism (e.g. 'abstract individualism') premised on essentialism tend, obviously, to distinguish the individual from society and give absolute priority to the former. In effect the individual is understood in terms of a pre-social essence, nature, or identity and on that basis s/he is invested with a quasi-spiritual autonomy. The individual becomes the origin and focus of meaning – an individuated essence which precedes and – in idealist philosophy – transcends history and society.

Reflecting here its religious antecedents, idealist philosophy marks off the domain of the spiritual as superior to, and the ultimate counter-image of, actual, historical, social, existence. It is not only that (as Nietzsche contended) the entire counterfeit of transcendence and of the hereafter has grown up on the basis of an impoverished life, but that transcendence comes to constitute an ideological mystification of the conditions of impoverishment from which it grew: impoverishment shifts from being its cause to its necessary condition, that required to pressure one's true (spiritual) identity into its true transcendent realisation. As Robbe-Grillet puts it, in the humanist tragic sense of life 'interiority always leads to transcendence . . . the pseudo-necessity of tragedy to a metaphysical beyond;' but at the same time it 'closes the door to any realist future' since the corollary of that beyond is a static, paralysed present.[26] The truth that people do not live by bread alone may then be appropriated ideologically to become the 'truth' that spiritual nourishment is an adequate substitute for bread and possibly even preferable to it. But most importantly, the *'revolutionary force of the ideal, which in its very unreality keeps alive the best desires of men amidst a bad reality'* is lost, displaced by ideals of renunciation and acquiescence.[27] Rebellious desire is either abdicated entirely or tamed in service to the cultural reification of 'man', the human condition, the human spirit and so on.

Marcuse, writing in 1936, was trying to explain the transition from liberalism to authoritarianism which Europe was witnessing. We may be unable to accept some of Marcuse's conclusions but the task he set himself then seems as urgent as ever. In one thing he was surely right: the essentialism of western philosophy, especially that of the idealist tradition, could be used to sanction that process whereby 'the soul was able to become a useful factor in the technique of mass domination when, in the epoch of authoritarian states, all available forces had to be mobilised against a real transformation of social existence'.[28] The attacks upon idealist culture by Brecht, Walter Benjamin and Theodore Adorno were made from similiar positions. In their very different ways these three writers engage with the materialist conception of subjectivity, one which, in so far as it retains the concept of essence, construes it not as that which is eternally fixed but as social potential materialising within limiting historical conditions. Conditions will themselves change – in part under the pressure of actualised potential – thus enabling new potentialities to unfold.

Arguably, to accept with Marx that Feuerbach was wrong 'to resolve the essence of religion into the essence of *man*', since 'the real nature of man is the totality of social relations', should be to dispense altogether with 'essence', 'nature' and 'man' as concepts implicated irredeemably in the metaphysic of determining origin.[29] Such at least is the implication of cultural materialism and that most famous of its formulations by Marx: 'The mode of production of material life conditions the social, political and intellectual life process in general'.[30] Consequently it is social being that determines consciousness, not the reverse.

In recent years the critique of essentialism has become even more searching partly in an attempt to explain its extraordinary recuperative power. Thus for Althusser humanism is characterised by two complementary and indissociable postulates: '(i) that there is a universal essence of man; (ii) that this essence is the attribute of "*each single individual*" who is its real subject' (the italicised phrase is a direct reference to Marx's sixth thesis on Feuerbach). Humanism gives rise to the concept of 'man' which, says Althusser, must be abolished: 'It is impossible to *know* anything about men except on the absolute precondition that the philosophical (theoretical) myth of man is reduced to ashes'.[31] Against humanism Althusser contends that 'The human subject is decentred, constituted by a structure which has no "centre" either, except in the imaginary misrecognition of the "ego", that is to say in the ideological formations where it finds recognition'.[32]

Before continuing, two general points are worth remarking. First, Althusser is here drawing on psychoanalytic theory whereas I shall not. What follows involves cultural materialist, Marxist and post-structuralist analysis of a different kind. Second, the controversy surrounding not just Althusser but the anti-humanism of Marxism, structuralism and post-structuralism generally has in part been due to a confusion of terms, and it has a long history. Thus Colin Wilson could declare in the fifties that he was an anti-humanist, yet his existentialist idealism is completely alien to the respective positions of, say, Althusser and Foucault. Indeed, according to those positions Wilson's own philosophy would be ineradicably humanist in virtue of its reliance on transcendent subjectivity. Wilson acknowledges quite explicitly that his is an idealism struggling to get back to its religious roots: 'Religion *must* be the answer'. And his definition of humanism includes, among other things, 'the values of the mass', 'scientific materialism' and 'progress' – all of which materialist anti-humanism might endorse, though not uncritically. Anti-humanism would also utterly dissociate itself from Wilson's absurd contention that humanism (thus defined) has engendered 'nothing but mass-boredom and frustration, and periodic outbreaks of war'.[33] Wilson is not an anti-humanist in either Althusser's or Foucault's sense; he is, rather, anti-humanitarian and anti-democratic and in this resembles his precursors – T. E. Hulme, Eliot and others. Probably it is pointless to try and rescue the term anti-humanism, especially since the important issues can better be focused by addressing a more fundamental division – of which the humanist/anti-humanist controversy is only a manifestation – namely, that between idealist and materialist conceptions of subjectivity.

Derrida has insisted that metaphysics is so deeply rooted in our discourses that there is no getting beyond it; perhaps in this he is too fatalistic.[34] Nevertheless his assertion is strikingly apt for the history of the essentialist humanism which has pervaded English studies and carried within it a residual metaphysic, one which makes for the ideological effacement of socio-cultural difference and historical context. It thereby denies or at least seeks to minimise the importance of material conditions of human existence for the forms which that existence takes. . . .

The main historical antecedents of this process of decentring have often been cited: Copernicus displaced man and his planet from their privileged place at the centre of the universe; Darwin showed that the human species is not the *telos* or goal of that universe; Marx displaced man from the centre of history while Freud displaced consciousness as the source of individual autonomy. Foucault adds the decentring effected by the Nietzschean genealogy (an addition which would appropriately challenge the suspiciously sequential coherence of the foregoing 'history' of decentring!): 'What is found at the historical beginning of things is not the inviolable identity of their origin; it is the dissension of other things. It is disparity'.[35]

Foucault identifies an 'epistemological mutation' of history not yet complete because of the deep resistance to it, a resistance, that is, to 'conceiving of difference, to describing separations and dispersions, to dissociating the reassuring form of the identical'.[36] He summarises his own task as one of freeing thought from its subjection to transcendence and analysing it 'in the discontinuity that no teleology would reduce in advance; to map it in a dispersion that no pre-established horizon would embrace; to allow it to be deployed in an anonymity on which no transcendental constitution would impose the form of the subject; to open it up to a temporality that would not promise the return of any dawn. My aim was to cleanse it of all transcendental narcissism'.[37] Transcendental narcissism validates itself in terms of teleology, the subject, the pre-established horizon;

against this Foucault's history charts discontinuity, anonymity, dispersion.

Barthes offers a similar emphasis. To speak positively of the decentred subject is never just to acknowledge his or her contradictions: 'It is a diffraction which is intended, a dispersion of energy in which there remains neither a central core nor a structure of meaning: I am not contradictory, I am dispersed'; 'today the subject apprehends himself *elsewhere*'.[38] This entails not only a non-centred conception of identity but, correspondingly, a non-centred form of political awareness: 'According to Freud ... one touch of difference leads to racism. But a great deal of difference leads away from it, irremediably. To equalize, democratize, homogenize – all such efforts will never manage to expel "the tiniest difference", seed of racial intolerance. For that one must pluralise, refine, continuously'. Sexual transgression is affirmed while recognising that it tends to carry within itself a limiting inversion of the normative regime being transgressed. The more radical alternative to sexual liberation through transgression is a release of sexuality from meaning. Then there would be for example not homosexuality but '*homosexualities*' 'whose plural will baffle any constituted, centred discourse'.[39]

This dimension of post-structuralist theory arouses justifiable suspicion for seeming to advance subjective decentring simply in terms of the *idea* of an anarchic refusal adequate unto itself, thereby recuperating anti-humanism in terms of the idealism it rejects and rendering the subject so completely dispersed as to be incapable of acting as any agent, least of all an agent of change. Equally though, this criticism itself runs the risk of disallowing the positive sense of the ideal cited earlier – that which in virtue of its present unreality affirms known potentialities from within existing, stultifying, social realities. Ideologically ratified, those 'realities' become not merely an obstacle to the realisation of potential, to the possibility of social change, but work to make both potential and change literally unthinkable. This is why, quite simply, a vision of decentred subjectivity, like any other vision of liberation, cannot be divorced from a critique of existing social realities and their forms of ideological legitimation. It is here that we might, finally, invoke an earlier emphasis in Barthes' work. In *Mythologies* he reminded us that the myth of the human condition 'consists in placing Nature at the bottom of History'; to thus eternalise the nature of man is to render the destiny of people apparently unalterable. Hence the necessity to reverse the terms, to find history behind nature and thereby reveal nature itself as an ideological construct preempting change.[40]

Perhaps this remains the most important objective in the decentring of man, one which helps make possible an alternative conception of the relations between history, society and subjectivity, and invites that '*affirmation* which *then determines the noncentre otherwise than as loss of the centre*'.[41] It is a radical alternative which, in the context of materialist analysis, helps vindicate certain objectives: not essence but potential, not the human condition but cultural difference, not destiny but collectively identified goals.

From Jonathan Dollimore, *Radical Tragedy* (Brighton, 1984), pp. 49, 53–4, 260–1, 54–6, 156–8, 56–9, 69, 253, 250–3, 269–71.

NOTES

[This chapter is not about *Macbeth* as such, but is important for its critique of the essentialist-humanist view of tragedy in which *Macbeth* has been a central text (see my discussion of Raymond Williams in the Introduction). I am grateful to Dr Dollimore for allowing me to take passages from diverse parts of his book so as to capture some of the main lines of his argument. Ed.]

1. John Fekete, *The Critical Twilight* (London, 1977), p. 195.

2. G. W. F. Hegel, *Philosophy of Mind*, trans. William Wallace (Oxford, 1971), p. 1.

3. A. C. Bradley, *Shakespearean Tragedy*, 2nd edn (London, 1905), p. 18; A. C. Bradley, *Oxford Lectures on Poetry*, 2nd edn (London, 1909), p. 86.

4. Bradley, *Oxford Lectures*, p. 292.

5. Bradley, *Shakespearean Tragedy*, pp. 38, 33.

6. Bradley, *Oxford Lectures*, pp. 71, 91.

7. Bradley, *Shakespearean Tragedy*, pp. 279, 25.

8. Wilbur Sanders, *The Dramatist and the Received Idea* (Cambridge, 1968), p. 109.

9. G. W. F. Hegel, *On Tragedy*, ed. Anne and Henry Paolucci (New York, 1962), pp. 71, 51, 91.

10. Lawrence Michel and Richard B. Sewall, *Tragedy: Modern Essays in Criticism* (Westport, Conn., 1963), pp. 121–3.

11. G. K. Hunter, *Dramatic Identities and Cultural Tradition* (Liverpool, 1978), p. 183; Bradley, *Shakespearean Tragedy*, p. 37.

12. Dorothea Krook, *Elements of Tragedy* (New Haven and London, 1969), pp. 8–9, 17.

13. John Tinsley, 'Tragedy and Christian Belief', *Theology* (March 1982), 100–2.

14. Raymond Williams, *Modern Tragedy* (London, 1979), pp. 202–3.

15. T. S. Eliot, *Selected Essays*, 3rd edn (London, 1951), pp. 112, 114.

16. William Archer, *The Old Drama and the New* (London, 1923), p. 134.

17. Eliot, *Selected Essays*, p. 111.

18. Archer, *The Old Drama and the New*, p. 20.

19. Jonas A. Barish, 'The New Theatre and the Old', in *Reinterpretations of Elizabethan Drama*, ed. Norman Rabkin (New York, 1969), p. 4.

20. T. S. Eliot, '*Ulysses*, Order and Myth', reprinted as 'Myth and Literary Classicism', in *The Modern Tradition*, ed. Richard Ellmann and Charles Fiedelson, Jr (New York, 1965), p. 681.

21. Eliot, *Selected Essays*, p. 185.

22. T. S. Eliot, *The Sacred Wood* (London, 1920), pp. 116–17.

23. Eliot, *Selected Essays*, pp. 139, 136–7; Dollimore's italics.

24. J. W. Lever, 'Shakespeare and the Ideas of His Time', *Shakespeare Survey*, 29 (1976), 85; Dollimore's italics.

25. Robert Paul Wolff, *The Poverty of Liberalism* (Boston, 1968), p. 142.

26. Alain Robbe-Grillet, 'Nature, Humanism and Tragedy', in *Snapshots and Towards a New Novel*, trans. Barbara Wright (London, 1965), pp. 81, 84.

27. Herbert Marcuse, *Negations*, trans. J. Shapiro (London, 1968), pp. 102, and 109–22; Dollimore's italics.

28. Ibid., p. 114.

29. Karl Marx, *Selected Writings in Sociology and Social Philosophy*, ed. T. B. Bottomore and Maximilien Rubel (Harmondsworth, 1963), p. 83.

30. Karl Marx, *Selected Works* (one volume) (London, 1968), p. 182.

31. Louis Althusser, *For Marx* (London, 1977), pp. 228–9.

32. Louis Althusser, *Lenin and Philosophy and Other Essays* (London, 1977), p. 201.

33. Colin Wilson, 'Beyond the Outsider', in *Declaration*, ed. Tom Maschler (London, 1957), pp. 36–46.

34. Jacques Derrida, *Positions*, trans. Alan Bass (London, 1981), p. 21.

35. Michel Foucault, *Language, Counter-Memory, Practice* (Ithaca and New York, 1977), p. 142.

36. Michel Foucault, *The Archaeology of Knowledge*, trans. A. M. Sheridan Smith (London, 1974), pp. 11–12.

37. Ibid., p. 203.

38. Roland Barthes, *Roland Barthes*, trans. Richard Howard (London, 1977), pp. 143, 168.

39. Ibid., p. 69; also pp. 64–5, 133.

40. Roland Barthes, *Mythologies*, trans. Annette Lavers (St Albans, 1973), p. 101.

41. Jacques Derrida, *Writing and Difference*, trans. Alan Bass (London, 1978), p. 292.

12

Radical Potential: 'Macbeth' on Film

GRAHAM HOLDERNESS

... Writing from within the embattled domain of 'Literature' teaching and criticism, we are likely to assume that any translation of a Shakespeare text into a 'live' dramatic form – theatrical performance, film adaptation, television production – will automatically constitute a progressive act. Such translation seems inevitably to entail a liberation of the *play*, a text for reproduction or recreation in performance, from the fetished holy writ of the *text*; and any move to challenge the hegemony of that dominant form of ideological oppression must, surely, be welcomed.

Theatrical, film and television productions have always been accorded a place and a potential value within the broad conspectus of a literary education: the question is what place, and what value? Are such things ancillary to the essential critical labour, marginal diversions to the study of texts? Traditional 'Literature' must keep them peripheral, since when they become a central focus they tend to displace the text from its central role in constituting the nature of the subject; tend to render the discipline itself unstable, open to question, vulnerable to change. Useful evidence of the tension created when film is introduced into the institution of Literature can be found in GCE O level examiners' reports (I offer a few instances from many examples):

> Imaginative interpretations of texts can be misleading. The visual impact of films and productions of plays was often stronger than the impact of Shakespeare's or Hardy's words.

> Films and stage-productions are not always entirely helpful. Lady Macduff bathing her son, Macbeth's soldiers attacking her maids, Lady Macbeth leaping from the battlements, Macbeth's mutilated body scattered across the stage, were so commonplace that it seemed fortunate that productions of *The Crucible* were less easily available.
>
> ... most candidates appeared to know *Macbeth* well. Some, however, were handicapped by having seen a film version ... candidates should remember that it is Shakespeare's text which is being examined.[1]

'Literature' here encounters 'Film' as a subversive influence to be resisted, marginalised or suppressed. Is the adoption of Shakespeare by the cinematic medium in educational practice, if not in the commercial cinema, inherently radical?

Catherine Belsey, in a very interesting article, proposes exactly the opposite: in her argument, both the literary text and a theatrical production under Elizabethan stage conditions are potentially productive of plurality of meaning, whereas films operate to close the plural work into a single dimension of significance:

> In the Elizabethan theatre there is no proscenium arch, no painted backdrop defining a setting in perspective, but a stage projected outwards into the auditorium, with the audience placed on at least three sides of it and possibly four. There is no single place to which the action is addressed and from which it is intelligible. The introduction after 1660 of the proscenium theatre with perspective backdrops radically changed the relationship between the audience and the stage ...
>
> ... Film is the final realisation of the project of perspective staging. The framed rectangle contains a world which is set out as the single object of the spectator's gaze, displayed in order to be known from a single point of view ... Through the intervention of the camera, which monitors what we see and therefore what we know, the film collects up meanings which may be lying around in the text, and streamlines them into one single, coherent interpretation which it fixes as inescapable. It arrests the play of possible meanings and presents its brilliant rectangle full of significance to and from a specific place, a single and at the same time inevitable point of view.[2]

This passage represents a body of opinion which forms, to my original thesis, the antithesis: that film is an inherently *conservative* medium, which inevitably exercises a despotic ideological control over the spectator's responses, closing off the work's potentiality for multiplicity of significance, depriving the audience of an opportunity to participate in a collaborative construction of meaning. 'Film', in the words of another writer, 'overwhelms the mind with a relentless progression of visual and auditory impulses ... all other arts liberate the imagination, film entraps it.'[3]

In terms of this latter view, the medium of film itself can only be an invisible, apparently innocent communicator of ideology. Like the naturalist stage, it purports to provide the spectator with a transparent window on to experience: isolated in the darkness of an auditorium she or he is overwhelmed with an enormous concentration of visual imagery insistently signifying its irreducible reality. Belsey offers as illustrations two films, both of which are said to offer ideology a free, unhampered passage: Joseph L. Mankiewicz's *Julius Caesar* (1953) transmits the liberal dilemma of a bourgeois-democratic society; while the *King Lear* (1970) of Peter Brook communicates a 'theoretical nihilism': '... like *Julius Caesar*, this film also makes a political statement: that the struggle for change, however heroic, is doomed in a world where all law, morality and justice are finally illusory'. Mankiewicz's film is of course a piece of thoroughgoing film naturalism, alternating close-ups of the main characters with long-shots of crowd scenes, all played against a 'realistic' Roman background. Belsey acknowledges, in an enthusiastic critique, that the cinematic techniques of *King Lear* are stylistically very different: she lists the grainy black-and-white photography, stylised acting, direct addresses to camera, lightning changes of focus, rapid superimpositions, violations of screen direction. She could have added the Brechtian titles, the absence of music, the distorted images, zoom-fades, blurred visions, surreal apparitions; the 'disjointed and staccato quality, elliptic camera-work, and violent mannerist cutting';[4] all devices which estrange the film's techniques from naturalism and from familiar screen conventions. Can a film constructed from such alienating, deconstructive devices really be a vehicle for the smooth and uninterrupted passage of ideology; can such discordant techniques really operate to naturalise ideology, obediently miming its chosen language?

Consider Brook's handling of a particularly complex dramatic moment, Gloucester's attempted suicide. Grigori Kozintsev in his film of the play felt that this scene was essentially a theatrical gesture, and avoided it by cutting. Brook, with Beckett and Jan Kott in the background, embraced the moment as a central thematic and dramatic focus of the work.

> The director duplicates in cinematic terms Shakespeare's blend of blatant stage artifice and imaginative reality ... a long shot shows

Edgar and Gloucester struggling along a flat plain. But then, in a series of tight, low-angle close-ups, Edgar and Gloucester seem to climb. The sound of the waves in the distance accords with Edgar's description, and following film convention it makes us imagine an off-screen reality. Set on 'the extremest verge', Gloucester bids farewell to poor Tom, and his final speech of despair is filmed in low-angle close-up . . . as he falls forward, however, Brook jolts us with an illusion-shattering cut to an extreme overhead long-shot. From this godlike perspective, we watch a tiny old man take a silent pratfall on a barren stretch of sand.[5]

The complex effects of this filmic montage can't adequately be summarised either in terms of Belsey's 'political statement', or of Jorgens's 'absurdist pantomime'. The director has certainly composed and edited his shots to expose the distinction between Gloucester's physical tumble and his psychological fall down mountains of the mind; and the final perspective is that of a god dispassionately watching a wanton boy killing flies. But the effect of, for example, the low-angle close-up of Gloucester's face (described by Jorgens as 'one of the most savagely beautiful shots of a human face ever put on film'), a frame from which the character towers over the spectator in the tragic dignity of suffering, is *complicated* but not *negated* by the jump-cut to an overhead long-shot of his pathetic fall. Moreover the fracturing of naturalist conventions increases the spectator's awareness of the camera as a constructive device, not a window opening on reality, but a mobile and changing point-of-view which can choose to record in a spirit of empathy or of alienation. The primary function of alienating devices, in this film or any other, is to intensify the viewer's awareness of the mechanisms by which this simulated reality is being produced; to impede the free transmission of ideology by discouraging unconscious, empathetic involvement and encouraging a vigilant and self-conscious curiosity, both about the object of the medium, and about the medium itself.

Belsey's identification of film with naturalist staging, though suggestive, is potentially misleading. Though the proscenium-arch perspective stage is very obviously a *selector* of reality, it can only *appear* to be an innocent *constitutor* of the reality: the spectator's point of vision is fixed, the access to the stage's simulated reality circumscribed, the window on to experience absolutely static. The film camera, by contrast, can do either: it can, like the proscenium arch, efface itself in a privileging of its object, constituting reality as objective in the illusionistic manner of naturalism; or it can, by violating those naturalist conventions, by emphasising and exploiting its mobility, call the spectator's attention to the mechanisms of its own perception. Without employing alienation devices, the naturalist stage can *only* offer itself as the *premise* of a simulated reality; the film can be seen to operate as a moving *commentary* on its object, releasing the viewer from the tyranny of empathetic illusion to a freer consideration of reality and of the artifice which produces it.

Considering Shakespeare films in the light of this most fundamental distinction in the whole of film theory – between naturalistic, illusionist cinema and its opposite – we can conclude that certain filmed adaptations of the plays operate simply as vehicles for the transmissions of ideology. Other films block, deflect or otherwise 'work on' ideology in order partially to disclose its mechanisms. The same method of evaluation will reveal which films are potentially more valuable for mobilisation in the educational context; and which can only work to reinforce and familiarise conventional attitudes to Shakespeare. Again, the object of this essay is not to attempt such evaluation across a wide range of films, but rather to suggest, with the help of particular illustrations, methods of procedure and analysis appropriate to such investigation.

In addition to describing the formal characteristics of the medium, some account must be taken, in however abstract a fashion, of the audience itself: which is not, after all, entirely created by the particular work of art it happens to be witnessing. A film of Shakespeare is never experienced in total vacuum, because of the ubiquity, the universality of Shakespeare as a cultural phenomenon. A film's 'arrested play of meanings' will enter into conflictual or co-operative relationship with certain ideological premises, certain cultural assumptions, certain definite levels of knowledge. The school students rebuked by the JMB examiners were witnessing a film *in the light of* some knowledge of the play as literary text. The film may be experienced in a context of other encounters with the play – a TV or theatrical production perhaps, or another film (most of the 'great' Shakespeare plays have been filmed several times). Or the film may simply reinforce or subvert an inherited cultural concept of 'Shakespeare' – the familiar associations of costume drama, perspective staging, unintelligible plots, projected delivery. It is this body of assumptions that an effective film transliteration is likely to subvert: clashing with the spectator's preconceptions to produce a liberating dialectic, to foster that very 'play of meanings' which art can press ideology to deliver. . . .

Akira Kurosawa's *Throne of Blood* (1957) is the most complete

translation of Shakespeare into film. The text is abandoned altogether, not even translated; the action shifted from medieval Scotland to feudal Japan; a western Renaissance tragedy becomes an
Oriental samurai epic. This most celebrated of all Shakespeare films
has been praised particularly for the completeness of its transformation of drama into cinema: 'the great masterpiece' (Peter Brook), 'the
finest of the Shakespeare movies' (Grigori Kozintsev). Critics have
stressed the *independence* of play and film: Frank Kermode called it
'an allusion to *Macbeth*', and Peter Brook asserted that it 'doesn't
come into the Shakespeare question at all'. J. Blumenthal calls it 'a
masterpiece in its own right', wholly liberated from 'the dreaded
literary media'.[6] Clearly, if play and film occupy entirely different
spaces and cannot even be compared, much less evaluated, against
one another: not only do the separate 'masterpieces' enjoy their
independent prestige, but the film is rendered incapable of violating
the integrity of 'Shakespeare', unable to interrogate or subvert the
play's immortal and immanent identity. If this proposition were
accepted, *Throne of Blood* would disappear from 'the Shakespeare
question' altogether and would offer the possibility of meaning only
in relation to Kurosawa's other work and to Japanese culture,
ideology and society.

The most substantial critical objection made against the film is that
it robs Shakespeare's play of its tragic form and style: 'Kurosawa's
Macbeth is not grand'; 'His crime is not against God but against
Society'; 'Kurosawa has betrayed the power of the play'.[7] In fact this
is clearly a fundamental aesthetic strategy of the film, which begins in
a style more epic than tragic, with a chorus commenting on the
images of a ruined castle and a grave: 'Behold within this place now
desolate stood once a mighty fortress, / Lived a proud warrior
murdered by ambition, his spirit walking still. / Vain pride, then as
now, will lead ambition to the kill.' The film's narrative is thus
framed by an artistic device which contains the story in an explicit
moral meaning offered for consideration, to an epic rather than a
dramatic audience. Epic detachment is also characteristic of the
film's visual style, which is largely structured by the conventions of
Japanese Noh drama. Acting and *mise-en-scène* are conventionalised
rather than naturalistic; 'Noh is ritual drama, and the world of the
Noh is both closed and artificial'. The camerawork, as Kurosawa
himself declared, entailed a deliberate avoidance of close-ups.[8] The
effect of this technique is detachment: 'the camera and chorus
maintain an aesthetic distance from the action';[9] or as Donald Richie

terms it, 'alienation': '. . . alienation is one of the effects of moving the camera back just as moving it forward suggests empathy. The full-shot reveals everything, . . . it disengages the viewer and allows him to see cause and effect'.[10]

What can this cinematic interpretation tell us about Shakespeare's *Macbeth?* To begin with, it locates the problem of regicide (*ge-koku-jo*) into a very specific historical and social context, parallel with Duncan's feudal Scotland but radically unlike Shakespeare's England or the modern world. The film displays a militaristic society with an elaborate code of loyalty, expressed in conventionalised social rituals: the intensely-stylised social intercourse of samurai and lord seeks to control the power and violence by which such a society exists. 'Ambition' in this society is not some eccentric personality-disorder, but a central historical contradiction: a natural extension of the militaristic violence which is both liberated and restrained by the feudal pattern of authority. 'What samurai does not want to be lord of a castle?' Washizu (Macbeth) asks Miki (Banquo). The question cannot be explained away in psychological terms, nor collapsed into a universalist moral system. It has meaning only within the historical world of the film. To adopt a similar perspective on *Macbeth* would entail a focus on the play's reconstruction of a distant society, observed not as a shadowy presage of the present, nor as a universal, providentially-established natural kingdom of the past. *Macbeth* opens with a startling contradiction: between the ugly, violent butchery described by the captain, in his account of Macbeth's killing of Macdonwald; and the elaborate rhetoric of chivalry and courtesy used by Duncan to control that power. Macbeth is bound to Duncan by that language of trust, loyalty, honour; but also by a social relationship which depends on a vulnerable and unstable division of authority and power. When Duncan declares Malcolm his successor (a declaration which indicates that this is *not* a hereditary dynasty) he is simultaneously creating a hierarchy and rendering it open to assault by suppressing the very power, vested in the thanes, which sustains his authority.

Critics have complained at the film's understanding of tragic 'inevitability' as social rather than psychological or supernatural: 'Washizu is given social and biological excuses for what can only be put down to unfathomable greed in Shakespeare's Macbeth'.[11] But it is evident that *both* Kurosawa's film *and* Shakespeare's play can be seen primarily as *social* tragedies, set within a distanced historical context in which social problems and contradictions can be rendered visible and fully intelligible to the audience's *curiosity*. Furthermore, tragedy narrated with such aesthetic detachment becomes 'epic'. The *tragedy* of Macbeth involves some degree of empathetic involvement by the spectator in the protagonist's experience; like Malcolm, we identify with Macbeth in order to live imaginatively through the knowledge of evil in a cathartic purgation. *Throne of Blood* denies the spectator that experience, and offers in its place, in the epic style, a detached scrutiny of certain actions and events within a certain social context. The choreographed artifice of Noh drama can certainly express a sense of constraint and predetermined destiny: but the artifice is visible, self-evident and self-conscious; the actors are acting out a stylised performance, not miming an inevitable process of psychological development. Again, it is valid to see *Macbeth* itself as an epic rather than a tragic drama. A performance of the play in Elizabethan stage conditions would have possessed certain qualities evident in the film (excluding of course the film's location sequences): bare sets, conventionalised acting, certain possibilities for detachment and alienation (consider Macbeth's self-reflexive characterisation of himself as a 'poor player'), and the acting-out of a well-known story the outcome of which is known beforehand. Even the soliloquies, so highly privileged by modern psychological interpretations, would not have been played as intense self-communings but as colloquies, dialogues between actor and audience. This is no mere academic speculation: Trevor Nunn's 1976 television production of *Macbeth* brings out these qualities of the play with startling distinctness: using a bare studio, actors visible *as* actors, nondescript costume, direct addresses to camera; all techniques which foreground the 'epic' rather than the 'tragic' dimension of the play.

I am not attempting to argue that Kurosawa has discovered and expressed the *true meaning* of Shakespeare's play: that would be to acknowledge that the text has an authentic, immanent meaning released by a particular act of interpretation. *Throne of Blood* is self-evidently *not* Shakespeare; and therein lies its incomparable value for strategic use in a radical exploration of the play. If the text can be reproduced in a virtually unrecognisable form, then the plurality of the text is proved beyond reasonable doubt. This bastard offspring, the play's *alter ego*, can then be brought back into conjunction with the text, to liberate some of its more radical possibilities of meaning. . . .

Film and television reproduction of Shakespeare are in essence no different from other forms of reproduction, in theatre or education: they have specific commercial and cultural functions within the economic and ideological apparatus of a bourgeois-democratic society. Spaces are created within that cultural apparatus for radical intervention, and such opportunities have to a limited extent been seized. The most promising space for cultural intervention remains, despite systematic attacks on the system, that of education; where film and television productions can be introduced into literature courses, posing fundamental cultural questions, liberating radical possibilities of meaning, and contributing to the much needed politicisation of the 'Shakespeare' institution.

From Graham Holderness, 'Radical Potentiality and Institutional Closure', in Jonathan Dollimore and Alan Sinfield (eds), *Political Shakespeare* (Manchester, 1985), pp. 182–7, 189–92, 199–200.

NOTES

[If 'the text' is an unstable construct at the best of times, what is the status of film versions of the bard? – Contentious, Graham Holderness shows. But Akira Kurosawa's *Throne of Blood*, by interpreting *Macbeth* not as a tragedy of Man but as an epic – encouraging attention to social problems and contradictions – may help readers to realise in the play a radical potential such as the previous two extracts have invoked. Ed.]

1. The three comments are from Joint Matriculation Board, *Examiners' Reports*, vol. 1, *Arts and Social Sciences*, in the years 1974 (p. 9), 1973 (p. 9) and 1977 (p. 9).

2. Catherine Belsey, 'Shakespeare and Film', *Literature/Film Quarterly*, 11 (Spring 1983).

3. S. D. Lawder, 'Film: Art of the Twentieth Century', *Yale Alumni Magazine* (May 1968), 33.

4. David Robinson, *Financial Times* (23 July 1971), quoted by Jack Jorgens, *Shakespeare on Film* (Bloomington, 1977), p. 244.

5. Jorgens, *Shakespeare on Film*, p. 240.

6. Peter Brook, 'Shakespeare on Three Screens', *Sight and Sound*, 34 (1965), 68; Grigori Kozintsev, *Shakespeare, Time and Conscience* (New York, 1966), p. 29; Frank Kermode, 'Shakespeare in the Movies', *New York Review of Books* (10 October 1972); J. Blumenthal, '*Macbeth* into Throne of Blood', *Sight and Sound*, 34 (1965), 191.

7. Donald Richie, *The Films of Akira Kurosawa* (Berkeley and Los

Angeles, 1965), p. 117; Ana Laura Zambrano, '*Throne of Blood*: Kurosawa's *Macbeth*', *Literature/Film Quarterly*, 2 (Summer 1974), 269; John Gerlach, 'Shakespeare, Kurosawa and *Macbeth*', *Literature/Film Quarterly*, 1 (Fall 1973), 352.

8. Richie, *Films of Akira Kurosawa*, pp. 117, 121.

9. Zambrano, '*Throne of Blood*', p. 16.

10. Richie, *Films of Akira Kurosawa*, p. 121.

11. Gerlach, 'Shakespeare, Kurosawa and *Macbeth*', p. 357.

Further Reading

STRUCTURALIST AND POSTSTRUCTURALIST READINGS

Harry Berger, 'Text Against Performance in Shakespeare: the example of *Macbeth*', in *The Power of Forms in the English Renaissance*, ed. Stephen Greenblatt (Norman, Oklahoma: Pilgrim Books, 1982).

An ambitious reconsideration of the relations between the play for reading and the play in the theatre; with a reading of *Macbeth* presenting 'the play's surface cosmology as a collective project of mystification' (p. 64) through which *all* the Scots justify themselves so as to cover for their anxieties about manliness. The palpability of the Witches may seem at odds with this, but they are merely 'shrunken figures of evil who are as comical as they are sinister' (p. 67).

James L. Calderwood, *If It Were Done: 'Macbeth' and tragic action* (Amherst: University of Massachusetts Press, 1986).

Reassertion of liberal-humane idea of the play, drawing upon René Girard's anthropological theory of violence and meaning in his *Violence and the Sacred*.

Kiernan Ryan, *Shakespeare*, Harvester New Readings (Hemel Hempstead: Harvester Wheatsheaf, 1989).

Ryan argues generally for the 'progressive potential' of Shakespeare, finding in a section on *Macbeth* 'an unrivalled arraignment of one of the mainsprings of modern western society: the ideology and practice of individualism'. Compare Eagleton, essay 4 in the present collection.

Leonard Tennenhouse, *Power on Display* (New York and London: Methuen, 1986).

A few pages on *Macbeth* shift discussion out of the 'character' mode, showing power appropriated and reappropriated.

Catherine Belsey, *Critical Practice* (London: Methuen, 1980).

Still a good place to start on modern critical method, with a couple of sharply focused pages on *Macbeth*.

HISTORICAL AND POLITICAL CONTEXTS

It is by no means simple to say what preoccupied people in earlier times;

several recent studies have shown the intricate relations of *Macbeth* with its historical context.

Michael Hawkins, 'History, Politics and *Macbeth*', in *Focus on 'Macbeth'*, ed. John Russell Brown (London: Macmillan, 1982).
A thorough and substantial account of 'the questions which concerned contemporaries' and 'how Shakespeare dealt with them', with a consistent awareness of the implications of relating a Shakespeare play to historical context.

David Norbrook, '*Macbeth* and the Politics of Historiography', in *Politics of Discourse: the literature and history of seventeenth-century England*, ed. Kevin Sharpe and Steven N. Zwicker (Berkeley: University of California Press, 1987).
Norbrook shows the significance of George Buchanan's account of Macbeth and Scottish history, and argues that Shakespeare follows neither Buchanan's hostility to unreasoning submission to hierarchy and tradition nor King James's line, but makes a distinctive negotiation of the complexities and embarrassments. The issue extends into questions of time, family, witchcraft and language.

Harry Berger, Jr, 'The Early Scenes of *Macbeth*: preface to a new interpretation', *English Literary History*, 47 (1980), 1–31.
Detailed account of Act 1, scene 2, showing how Duncan's Scotland is already disturbed. We see 'the plight of the king in this society: the more his subjects do for him, the more he must do for them; the more he does for them, feeding their ambition and their power, the less secure can he be of his mastery' (pp. 24–5).

Stuart Clark, 'Inversion, Misrule and the Meaning of Witchcraft', *Past and Present*, 87 (1980), 98–127.
A key contextual essay which aims to locate the mentality within which the inversion of normative imagery in witchcraft made sense. A principle of contrariety was believed to inform all things, and in the body politic also disorder was presented as contrariety. This approach was used, for instance by King James, to legitimate established authority and demonise dissidence.

Stephen Greenblatt, 'Shakespeare and the Exorcists', in Greenblatt, *Shakespearean Negotiations: the circulation of social energy in Renaissance England* (Oxford: Clarendon, 1988).
This essay about exorcism and *King Lear* does not discuss *Macbeth*, but its substantial handling of rival notions of the sacred has diverse implications for our understanding of the supernatural in the period.

Keith Thomas, *Religion and the Decline of Magic* (Harmondsworth: Penguin, 1973).
Full of fascinating documentation on how Shakespeare's contemporaries thought about ghosts, witches, prophecies, conjuring, religion and authority.

Alan Sinfield, *Faultlines: cultural materialism and the politics of dissident reading* (Berkeley: University of California Press, 1991).

Includes chapters commenting on political contexts of *Macbeth* and other writings of the time, with particular attention to contemporary religious ideas and to the present-day implications of the study of Shakespeare.

Kathleen McLuskie, *Renaissance Dramatists* (Hemel Hempstead: Harvester Wheatsheaf, 1989).
Supplies valuable context of social conditions, especially those in which plays were performed.

GENDER AND PSYCHOANALYSIS

Studies oriented around gender and psychoanalysis tend to divide into those which assume that there are healthy ways for men and women, respectively, to develop, and those that argue that these matters are social arrangements. Of the following, Berg and Berry, McLuskie, Jardine and Callaghan fall broadly into the latter, the remainder (listed first) into the former.

Coppélia · Kahn, *Man's Estate* (Berkeley: University of California Press, 1981).
A chapter on Macbeth in this psychoanalytic study presents him as suffering from an unfinished, not fully individuated, manly identity; hence his dependence on women and rivalries with men.

Carolyn Asp, '"Be bloody, bold and resolute": tragic action and sexual stereotyping in *Macbeth*', *Studies in Philology*, 78 (1981), 153–69.
Macbeth and Lady Macbeth are raised to the level of tragedy by 'the conflict between the [masculine and feminine] roles they think they must play to actualize the self and achieve their destiny, and the limits imposed by both nature and society' (p. 169).

Carolyn Ruth Swift Lenz, Gayle Greene and Carol Thomas Neely (eds), *The Woman's Part* (Urbana: University of Illinois Press, 1980).
Includes Joan Larsen Klein, 'Lady Macbeth: "Infirm of purpose"', and Madelon Gohlke, '"I wooed thee with my sword": Shakespeare's tragic paradigms'. The editors say the special project of feminist critics is to find women characters to be 'hardly the saints, monsters, or whores their critics have often perceived them to be. Like the male characters the women are complex and flawed, like them capable of passion and pain, growth and decay' (p. 5).

Richard P. Wheeler, *Shakespeare's Development and the Problem Comedies* (Berkeley: University of California Press, 1981).
Wheeler discusses psychological tensions in Shakespeare's art; including some pages on Macbeth's quest for manhood and on fear of women in *Macbeth*.

Robert Kimbrough, 'Macbeth: the prisoner of gender', *Shakespeare Studies*, 16 (1983), 175–90.
Macbeth does not achieve full humanity, which means not being crudely masculine.

Richard Horwitch, 'Integrity in Macbeth: the search for the "single state of man"', *Shakespeare Quarterly*, 29 (1978), 365–73.

'A sense of wholeness, completeness, or coherence has from the first represented the ideal but unattainable condition both of Scotland and of most of its inhabitants ... it is what Macduff possesses and what Macbeth, more than anyone else, lacks' (p. 366).

Christine Berg and Philippa Berry, '"Spiritual Whoredom": an essay on female prophets in the seventeenth century', in *1642: literature and power in the seventeenth century*, ed. Francis Barker *et al.* (Colchester: University of Essex, 1981).
  The Witches related to seventeenth-century anxiety about prophecy as a 'feminine' and revolutionary discourse.

Kathleen McLuskie, 'The Patriarchal Bard: feminist criticism and Shakespeare: *King Lear* and *Measure for Measure*', in *Political Shakespeare*, ed. Jonathan Dollimore and Alan Sinfield (Manchester: Manchester University Press, 1985).
  A critique of essentialist feminism, arguing that feminist criticism of *Measure for Measure* (for instance) 'is restricted to exposing its own exclusion from the text' (p. 97).

Lisa Jardine, *Still Harping on Daughters: women and drama in the age of Shakespeare* (Hemel Hempstead: Harvester Wheatsheaf, 1983).
  A vigorous and well documented account of the lives of women in Shakespeare's time with many references to the drama but only a few to *Macbeth*.

Dympna Callaghan, *Woman and Gender in Renaissance Tragedy* (Hemel Hempstead: Harvester Wheatsheaf, 1989).
  A stimulating and sophisticated discussion, mainly of *King Lear, Othello* and plays of John Webster, with occasional references to *Macbeth*.

SHAKESPEAREAN INSTITUTIONS

In the Jacobean theatre, through the centuries and in theatre and education systems today, *Macbeth* necessarily reaches audiences and readers through institutions.

Jonathan Bate, *Shakespearean Constitutions: politics, theatre, criticism 1730–1830* (Oxford: Clarendon, 1989).
  'If one tragedy were to be singled out for its political importance throughout the period from 1760 to 1830, it would have to be *Macbeth*' (p. 88). This densely detailed account of the deployment of Shakespeare in political disputes refers particularly to *Macbeth* in pp. 84–97; and there are interesting illustrations of cartoonists' use of the play.

Mary Jacobus, '"That Great Stage Where Senators Perform": *Macbeth* and the politics of Romantic theater', *Studies in Romanticism*, 22 (1983), 353–87.
  How Romantic poets and critics linked *Macbeth* to attitudes towards the French Revolution and poetic genius.

Stephen Orgel, 'The Authentic Shakespeare', *Representations*, 21 (Winter 1988), 1–25.
  Critics are deluded in attempts to establish *the* Shakespeare text, especially

since plays have always been adjusted in performance; exemplified from Garrick's 1744 production of *Macbeth* and eighteenth-century illustrations. It all depends what you mean by 'authenticity'!

George Winchester Stone, Jr, 'Garrick's Handling of *Macbeth*', *Studies in Philology*, 38 (1941); reprinted in *Shakespeare: 'Macbeth': a Casebook*, ed. John Wain (London: Macmillan, 1968).

Indicates the striking extent to which *Macbeth* was rewritten in the seventeenth and eighteenth centuries.

Marvin Rosenberg, *The Masks of Macbeth* (Berkeley: University of California Press, 1978).

Long and detailed account, scene by scene, of the play as a stage event, with many references to records of performances.

In *Political Shakespeare*, ed. Jonathan Dollimore and Alan Sinfield (Manchester: Manchester University Press, 1985): essays by Sinfield on the education system and the Royal Shakespeare Company.

Gary Taylor, *Reinventing Shakespeare: a cultural history from the Restoration to the present* (London: Hogarth Press, 1990).

Brisk, rather close-up account of the Shakespeare industry; chapter 6 is about events and publications of the year 1986.

Raymond Williams, *Modern Tragedy*, revised edn (London: New Left Books, 1979).

Part one traces concepts of tragedy to their sources and proposes a radical alternative conception (not specifically about *Macbeth*; discussed in the introduction to the present volume).

Jonathan Dollimore, *Radical Tragedy*, 2nd edn (Hemel Hempstead: Harvester Wheatsheaf, 1989).

Parts of this study of the concept of tragedy are in the present volume; the second edition has a new Introduction discussing recent trends in criticism.

TWO OTHER COLLECTIONS OF DIVERSE APPROACHES TO SHAKESPEARE

John Drakakis (ed), *Alternative Shakespeares* (London and New York: Methuen, 1985).

Jean E. Howard and Marion F. O'Connor (eds), *Reproducing Shakespeare* (New York and London: Methuen, 1987).

Notes on Contributors

Janet Adelman is Professor of English, University of California, Berkeley. Author of *The Common Liar: An Essay on 'Antony and Cleopatra'* (New Haven, 1973), and important essays on Shakespeare and psychoanalysis, including '"Anger's My Meat": Feeding, Dependency, and Aggression in *Coriolanus*', in *Representing Shakespeare: New Psychoanalytic Essays*, ed. Murray M. Schwartz and Coppélia Kahn (Baltimore, 1980); and '"This Is and Is Not Cressid": the Characterisation of Cressida', *The (M)other Tongue: essays in feminist psychoanalytic interpretation*, ed. Shirley Nelson Garner, Claire Kahane and Madelon Sprengnether (Ithaca and London, 1985).

Catherine Belsey is Professor of English Literature and Chair of the Centre for Critical and Cultural Theory at the University of Wales, Cardiff. Her publications include *Critical Practice* (London and New York, 1980); *The Subject of Tragedy: Identity and Difference in Renaissance Drama* (London and New York, 1985); *John Milton: Language, Gender, Power* (Oxford and New York, 1988); and *The Feminist Reader: Essays in Gender and the Politics of Literary Criticism* (ed. with Jane Moore, London and New York, 1989).

Jonathan Dollimore is a Reader at the University of Sussex. Author of *Radical Tragedy: Religion, Ideology and Power in the Drama of Shakespeare and his Contemporaries* (2nd edn, Hemel Hempstead, 1989); and of several essays on sexuality, including 'Sexuality, Subjectivity and Transgression: the Jacobean Connection', *Renaissance Drama*, new series, 17 (1986), 53–81. Editor (with Alan Sinfield) of *Selected Plays of John Webster* (Cambridge, 1983); and (with Alan Sinfield) of *Political Shakespeare: New Essays in Cultural Materialism* (Manchester, 1985). Dollimore has just completed a new book: *Sexual Dissidence* (Oxford, 1991).

Terry Eagleton is Professor of English at the University of Oxford. Among his books are *Criticism and Ideology: a Study in Marxist Critical Theory* (London, 1976); *Walter Benjamin or Towards a Revolutionary Criticism* (London, 1981); *The Rape of Clarissa* (Oxford, 1982); *Literary Theory:*

An Introduction (Oxford, 1983); *William Shakespeare* (Oxford, 1986); *Against the Grain* (London, 1986); *The Ideology of the Aesthetic* (Oxford, 1990).

Malcolm Evans's book *Signifying Nothing: Truth's True Contents in Shakespeare's Text* (1986) has recently been published in a second edition with a fighting conclusion questioning the achievement of recent critical work on Shakespeare (New York and London, 1989). He has an essay, 'Deconstructing Shakespeare's Comedies', in *Alternative Shakespeares*, ed. John Drakakis (London and New York, 1985).

Marilyn French is an author and critic. Her novels include *The Women's Room* (London, 1978), *The Bleeding Heart* (1980) and *Her Mother's Daughter* (1987); she has also published *The Book as World: James Joyce's 'Ulysses'* (Cambridge, Mass., 1976), *Shakespeare's Division of Experience* (London, 1982) and *Beyond Power: On Women, Men and Morals* (London, 1985).

Sigmund Freud (1856–1939) was the father (*sic*) of psychoanalysis, still often drawn upon by contemporary literary critics.

Jonathan Goldberg is Sir William Osler Professor of English Literature at the Johns Hopkins University. He is author of *Endlesse Worke: Spenser and the Structures of Discourse* (Baltimore and London, 1981); *James I and the Politics of Literature* (Baltimore and London, 1983); *Voice Terminal Echo: Postmodernism and English Renaissance Texts* (London and New York, 1986); *Writing Matter: From the Hands of the English Renaissance* (Stanford, 1990).

Graham Holderness is Head of Drama at Roehampton Institute. His publications include *Shakespeare's History* (Dublin, 1985); *Shakespeare: the Play of History*, with Nick Potter and John Turner (London, 1987); *Hamlet* (Milton Keynes, 1987); *Richard II* (Harmondsworth, 1989); *Shakespeare: Out of Court*, with Nick Potter and John Turner (London, 1990). He is the editor of *The Shakespeare Myth* (Manchester, 1988).

Steven Mullaney is Professor of English at the University of Ann Arbor, Michigan. His new-historicist work is published in *The Place of the Stage: License, Play and Power in Renaissance England* (Chicago, 1988).

Alan Sinfield is Professor of English at the University of Sussex. Co-editor, with Jonathan Dollimore, of *Political Shakespeare* (Manchester, 1985); editor of *Society and Literature 1945–1970* (London, 1983); author of *Literature in Protestant England 1560–1660* (London, 1983), *Alfred Tennyson* (Oxford, 1986), *Literature, Politics and Culture in Postwar Britain* (Oxford and Berkeley, 1989), *Faultlines: Cultural Materialism and the Politics of Dissident Reading* (to be published in 1991–2 by University of California Press).

Peter Stallybrass is Professor of English and chair of Cultural Studies at the University of Pennsylvania. Co-author with Allon White of *The Politics* *and Poetics of Transgression* (Ithaca and London, 1986), he has edited with David Kaston a collection of essays on Renaissance drama entitled *Staging the Renaissance* (London and New York, 1991). His *Embodied Politics: Discourses of Enclosure and Transgression in Early Modern England* is to be published by Routledge in 1991.

Index

absolutism, *see* law and order, the
  state
Adams, R., 10
Adelman, J., 6
Adorno, T., 144
Althusser, L., 105, 145
ambiguity, *see* equivocation
Archer, W., 140–1
Aristotle, 117
Artaud, A., 76
author, the, 10, 79, 93, 103

Bacon, F., 125
Bakhtin, M., 5
Barish, J., 141
Barthes, R., 147–8
Bayley, J., 133
Beckett, S., 153
Belsey, C., 7, 8, 72, 152–4
Benjamin, W., 144
Berger, H., 95, 105
Bible (quoted), 29, 35–6, 130–1;
  see religion
Blumenthal, J., 156
Bodin, J., 27, 36
Booth, W., 133
Bradley, A. C., 2–4, 6–7, 133,
  137–9, 142–3
Brathwait, R., 80
Brecht, B., 4, 140, 144, 153
Brook, Peter, 153–4, 156
Brooks, C., 21
Buchanan, G., 126–8, 130–2
Buckingham, Duke of, 26
Bullough, G., 92

Castle of Perseverance, The, 81,
  86
Charles I, 122
Cheeke, Sir J., 110
Christianity, *see* religion
church, the, 114, 122; *see* religion
Clark, S., 27
Coleridge, S. T., 113
conservatism, 132–4
Copernicus, 146
cultural materialism, 9–10, 130–4,
  137, 143–8, 159
Curry, W. C., 25, 33

Dante, 142
Darwin, C., 146
Davenant, Sir W., 131
Derrida, J., 12, 146, 148
dissidence, *see* rebellion
Dollimore, J., 4, 7–9
Donne, J., 142
Douglas, M., 26

Eagleton, T., 5–8
education, 10–12, 76–7, 151–2,
  155, 159
Eliot, T. S., 140–3
Elizabeth I, 26–7, 122
equivocation, 47–8, 65–6, 69–77,
  92–9, 103–5, 108–19, 131
essentialist humanism, *see*
  humanism
Essex, Earl of, 123
Evans, M., 7, 8
Everyman, 83–4

evil, 5, 23, 27, 30, 72–3, 76, 121–2, 128, 131–2, 134, 138

family, *see* gender and sexuality
Fekete, J., 136–7
film, 9–10, 151–9
Forster, E. M., 3
Fortescue, Sir A., 26
Foucault, M., 145–6
Fraunce, A., 112, 114
French, M., 4–5, 8
Freud, S., 4, 5, 146–7; *see* psychoanalysis

Gardner, H., 19
Garnet, Father, 113–14
gender and sexuality, 4–6, 14–67, 80, 103–5, 163–4
god(s), 4, 18, 27–30, 34–6, 81, 122, 125–6, 136–40; *see* religion
Goldberg, J., 7–8, 105
Gowrie, 112–13
Gowrie, Earl of, 108, 112
Greville, F., 139
Guattari, F., 89–90
Gunpowder Plot, 109, 112–13, 124, 126–7, 132

Hegel, G. W. F., 137–8
Heilman, R., 23
Henry VIII, 110, 122
Heywood, T., 85–7
history, new historicism, 8–9, 105, 121–34, 143–8, 157–8, 162–3
Holderness, G., 9–10
Holinshed, R., 8, 14, 28–9, 31–2, 42–3, 92–6, 111–12, 129
homosexuality, 147
Hulme, T. E., 146
humanism, anti-humanism, 7, 79–81, 85–90, 136–40, 143–8; *see* cultural materialism
Hunter, G. K., 127–8, 139

idealism, 137, 143–4
individualism, 49–50, 79–90, 133, 140, 143–8

Ireland, 123, 132
Irigaray, L., 104

Jack, J., 35
James VI and I, 8, 21, 27–9, 34, 36, 41, 96–105, 108–9, 113–15, 119, 122, 124–34
James, T., 114
Jameson, F., 96
Johnson, N., 26
Johnson, S., 57
Jonson, B., 96, 99–103, 142
Jorgens, J., 154

Kermode, F., 92
Kett, R., 111
Knight, G. W., 21, 74
Knights, L. C., 72
Kott, J., 153
Kozintsev, G., 153, 156
Krook, D., 139
Kurosawa, A., *Throne of Blood*, 10, 155–8
Kyd, T., 84

language, 6–8, 14, 22, 26, 33, 46–51, 59, 61, 69–77, 81–8; *see* equivocation
Larner, C., 27
law and order, 8–9, 15–20, 23, 27–9, 33–4, 46–50, 55, 65–7, 70–2, 98–105, 121–2, 132–3; *see* rebellion, the state
Lawder, S. D., 152–3
Leavis, F. R., 85–6
Lever, J. W., 142
liberalism, 79–81, 133–4, 153; *see* humanism
literature, literary criticism, 8–12, 35–7, 46–7, 65–6, 76–7, 85–90, 126, 132–4, 136–48, 151–2, 155, 158–9; *see* education

Macfarlane, A., 25
Macherey, P., 77
Machiavelli, 142
man, 4, 7, 48–50, 79–81, 86, 136–40, 142–8; *see* gender and sexuality

Mankiewicz, J. L., 153
manliness, *see* gender and sexuality
Marcuse, H., 144
Marlowe, C., 81–3
Marx, K., 4, 49–50, 144–6
Mary Queen of Scots, 41, 104–5,
   122, 127–8
metaphysics, 136–40, 143–8; *see*
   religion
Middleton, T., 96
Milton, J., 80–1
Montaigne, M., 142
Moretti, F., 98
Muir, K., 71, 77, 97, 117, 131–2
Mullaney, S., 8–9, 97–8
Murray, W. A., 35–6

nature, 4–5, 8, 15–16, 50, 65–7,
   70–3, 108–9, 132, 144
Newbolt Report, 76
Nietzsche, F., 143, 146
Nunn, T., 158

order, *see* law and order
Orgel, S., 96

Paul, H. N., 126
poststructuralism, 6–8, 143–8, 161
protestantism, 114, 124–5; *see*
   religion
psychoanalysis, 6, 53–68, 89–90,
   114, 145, 163; *see* Freud
Puttenham, G., 111, 117–18

Raymond, St, 114
readers and reading, 9–11, 35–7,
   43, 46, 75–7, 85–90, 126, 128,
   130–4, 152–3
realism, 81–8, 140–3, 152–3; *see*
   Brecht
rebellion, 108–19, 121–4, 126–8
religion, *see* the Bible, the church,
   god(s), metaphysics,
   protestantism, Roman
   Catholicism
Revenger's Tragedy, The, 141–2
Ribner, I., 132
Richie, D., 156–7
Robbe-Grillet, A., 144

Rogers, D., 80
Roman Catholicism, 112–14, 124;
   see Gunpowder Plot, religion
Rose, M., 31
Rowe, N., 77
Royal Shakespeare Company, 10
Russell, W., *Educating Rita,*
   1–12

St Bartholomew's Massacre, 123
Samson, A., 27
Sanders, W., 21, 138
Scotland, 5, 8, 14–15, 22, 27–30,
   41, 66–7, 104–5, 108, 113,
   126–8, 157
Scruton, R., 133
Seneca, 142
Sewell, R. B., 138–9
Shakespeare, Cymbeline, 54;
   Hamlet, 53–4, 87–8; *Henry V,*
   123; *1 Henry VI,* 32; *2 Henry
   VI,* 109; *Julius Caesar,* 153;
   King Lear, 7–8, 14, 17, 55, 138,
   153–4; *Measure for Measure,*
   48; *Othello,* 14, 19, 85–6;
   Richard II, 123; *Tempest, The,*
   51, 67; *Troilus and Cressida,*
   50
sign, the, *see* language
soliloquy, 79–88, 158
sources, 92–105, 130; *see*
   Holinshed
Spalding, T. A., 25
Spenser, E., 127
Stallybrass, P., 5, 8
state, the, 8–9, 36, 115, 118,
   121–34, 157; *see* law and order
structuralism, 6–7, 161
subjectivity, 47–8, 51, 79–90

television, 151, 155, 158–9
text, the, 7–9, 43, 57, 69–77,
   92–105, 130–1, 151, 155, 158;
   see language, sources
theatre, 8–10, 47, 109, 131,
   151–4, 158, 164–5; *see* realism
Thomas, K., 25
Tillyard, E. M. W., 143
Tinsley, J., 140

tragedy, 1–4, 9–11, 132–4,
    136–40, 156–8
treason, *see* rebellion

Wayne, D., 9
Williams, R., 2–4, 9, 81, 140
Wilson, C., 146

Wiseman, J., 124–5
witchcraft and witches, 5–6, 14,
    25–37, 46–8, 50, 54–8, 123,
    131
Wolff, R. P., 143
women, *see* gender and sexuality